SPELLING IMPROVEMENT
A PROGRAM FOR SELF-INSTRUCTION

SPELLING IMPROVEMENT

A PROGRAM FOR SELF-INSTRUCTION
SECOND EDITION

PATRICIA M. FERGUS
University of Minnesota

McGRAW-HILL BOOK COMPANY
New York St. Louis San Francisco Düsseldorf
Johannesburg Kuala Lumpur London Mexico Montreal
New Delhi Panama Rio de Janeiro
Singapore Sydney Toronto

SPELLING IMPROVEMENT:
A PROGRAM FOR
SELF-INSTRUCTION

1 2 3 4 5 6 7 8 9 0   KPKP   7 9 8 7 6 5 4 3

This book was set in News Gothic by Monotype Composition
Company, Inc. The editors were David Edwards, Harriet B. Malkin,
and James R. Belser; the designer was Ben Kann; and the
production supervisor was Sally Ellyson.
The printer and binder was Kingsport Press, Inc.

Library of Congress Cataloging in Publication Data

Fergus, Patricia M
    Spelling improvement.

    1.   English language—Orthography and spelling.
2.   Vocabulary.   I.   Title.
PE1143.F4   1973   428'.1   72-7049
ISBN 0-07-020469-1
ISBN 0-07-020468-3 (pbk.)

Contents

Preface   *vii*
Introduction   *ix*

Part One   SOUND AND SPELLING

Chapter 1   Pronunciation and Enunciation   *3*
2   Prefixes   *13*
3   Syllabication   *21*
4   Silent Letters   *35*
5   Vowel Stress   *41*
6   Sound-alike Suffixes   *51*

Part Two   MEANING AND SPELLING

7   The "Seed" Roots   *73*
8   Homonyms   *79*
9   Similar Word   *91*

Part Three   RULES AND SPELLING

10   Doubling the Final Consonant   *103*
11   The Final *E*   *113*
12   The Final *Y*   *123*
13   *IE* or *EI*   *131*
14   Plurals   *141*
15   Possessives   *151*
16   *LY* and *OUS*   *159*

Appendix A   Guidelines for Syllabication   *169*
B   Test Answers   *179*

Index   *193*

Preface

The second edition of this book has not departed from the principles of the first. Sound and meaning still play important roles in the process of spelling, and syllabication is still a good method for spelling familiar and unfamiliar words. The audience, too, remains the same. Generally, anyone who has a basic knowledge of the English language, and who can read and understand high school material, can read this text. And again, it can be adopted for a number of courses or independent study in high school, college and university, technical and trade schools, for use in educational programs in industry, business, government, and the military, or for use by any person who is motivated to improve his spelling.

Since the original edition appeared, however, some programming emphases have changed. This edition has therefore been completely reprogrammed to offer the student a new and challenging program: one in which behavioral objectives are stated for each chapter, one in which the user becomes aware, perhaps for the first time, of the whys and wherefores of good spelling, and one in which he applies what he learns. Also included in this edition are a far greater number of common and useful words as well as much more material on the etymology and structure of words, closely linking sound, meaning, and derivation.

The plan of the text makes it easy to adopt for classroom or study situations. The diagnostic pretests allow for bypassing chapters or working parts or all of the chapters as needed; the reviews supply a device for immediate testing; and the posttests serve the purpose of final testing.

An early version of this edition was tested in five selected schools, and the results were gratifying: Those finishing the program reduced their initial misspellings by seventy-five to eighty percent. Helpful comments from these students and their instructors made possible the present revised edition. I would like to acknowledge my gratitude, therefore, to these participating schools: Minnetonka High School, Excelsior, Minnesota; University City Senior High School, St. Louis; University of California/ Davis; Citrus College, California; and Lansing Community College, Michigan.

I would also like to thank the reviewers for their comments on the first edition and, in particular, Danny Langdon for his concrete suggestions and comments on both the first edition and the early version of the second.

Patricia M. Fergus

Introduction

THE ENGLISH WRITING SYSTEM

A writing system develops chiefly from attempts to standardize and innovate and from the political and educational
movements rather than from the linguistic process itself.
The English language has had an interesting development.
It was introduced in its earliest form from about the
middle of the fifth century by the Angles, Saxons, and
tribes from the northern part of Germany. These invaders
eventually founded kingdoms of their own, and from the
language of these Teutonic settlers developed the national
tongue. This Anglo-Saxon period, usually called "the Old
English period," extended until about 1100, when "the
Middle English period" began and which continued until
1500.

Of the three English periods—Old, Middle, and Modern
—the Middle period had the most effect on the writing
system as we know it today. There were gradual changes
in spelling to correspond better with various sounds.
There were sometimes several different developments of
phonemes which produced striking inconsistencies in modern English spelling, one of the most interesting yet
plaguing being *gh* (*through, rough, caught*).

From the twelfth century until well into the fourteenth,
many who wrote in English were extremely proficient in
French and brought many of the aspects of the French
language into English. For example, they borrowed the
French *ou* to replace the English *u* (as in *house* or *found*);
they borrowed whole words from the French; and they re-
placed many English characters with those from the
French.

Greek words were also borrowed during this period, and

although the Greek alphabet was related historically to the Latin alphabet, it was different enough to cause some problems. The Greek letters had to be represented by Roman letters, and in this representation decisions had to be made about the original or altered pronunciation and spelling. The familiar silent *p* at the beginning of such words as *psychology* and *pneumonia* or the "f" sound of *ph* in *philosophy* and *sophomore* can be linked to this period of borrowing from the Greek.

In the latter part of the Middle English period Latin loan words remained virtually unchanged, resulting in the addition of more rules to those already in use from Old English and French. An interesting point concerning Latin and French during this period of development is the spelling of several English suffixes. *Able* and *ible*, which often cause spelling difficulties today, were the French spellings from the Latin *abilis* or *ibilis*, the choice of which depended on the stem vowel of the Latin verb. Two other suffixes, *ance* and *ence*, are derived from the Latin verb endings *antem* and *entem,* but they have no relationship to phonological or grammatical systems of English today. Not only do we have problems with suffixes, but we also have silent letters which have either carried over from the Old English period or which were put back into words like dou*b*t and de*b*t by scholars who wanted the Latin derivation to be apparent.

The period generally from about 1350 to 1550 is considered the transition from Middle to Modern English, and it is in this stage that we have the Great Vowel Shift. Here the long stressed vowels moved forward in the mouth; for example, the *i* which was pronounced as a long e became the I that we know today as the personal pronoun. It was also at this time that the printing houses (printing having been brought into England by William Caxton in the midst of the shift) endeavored to standardize the spelling of many words and conventions, such as the initial and medial use of *i,* the final use of *y,* and the reduction of double consonants, but at the same time tended to retain some of the Middle English spelling. What resulted is obvious today: Some of our biggest problems in spelling are due to the variance between pronunciation and graphic presentation.

Linguistic research has shown, however, that a greater proportion of the English language is more phonetic than we realize. And it is this point that is important here. We *can* spell correctly. True, there are words that may perplex us for a while, but with so many helpful guides there is no reason why we should misspell many words.

REASONS FOR POOR SPELLING

One reason, touched on in the previous section, has to do with the words themselves. There are silent letters that must be included in the graphic presentation; there are suffixes that sound alike (*able-ible, ary-ery, ance-ence*) that must be selected for appropriate root words; there are vowels with slight or hardly any stress that must be correctly identified. There are also complete words that sound exactly alike (homonyms), so they must be distinguished by their meanings. For instance, the sets *cite-site-sight* and *principal-principle* have a single pronunciation but many meanings, and it is these definitions that tell you which to choose.

Another reason is that we do not pronounce words clearly and distinctly. We may add or omit syllables, or we may slur vowels or consonants, or even syllables. In other words, our carelessness can be a major cause of poor spelling. A reason closely allied to this is faulty discrimination, visual or auditory. This, again, can be carelessness, not even trying to see or hear what is contained in the word.

Lastly, there are many words that a few simple rules will take care of, such as the doubling of the final consonant in *beginning* or *equipped,* the absence of the final e in *desirous,* or the presence of the e in *advantageous.*

NEED FOR CORRECT SPELLING

The answer to the question posed by some students, "Why should I bother to spell correctly?" is obvious in the number of red marks on high school and college term papers, research papers, even theses, in the number of application forms turned down by prospective employers, and in the promotion that does not come as promptly as one wishes. The most important reason for correct spelling is one that is often overlooked or simply ignored: clear communication. Misspelled words can break the continuity or flow of ideas, and in this process they can and often will disconcert and irk the reader. The result will usually be the alienation of the reader, something no writer can afford.

PURPOSE OF THE BOOK

This text is designed to help any individual who misspells words for a variety of reasons to *improve* his spelling.

Since the primary emphases are on pronunciation, meaning of words, and syllabication, the chapters have been grouped together into three parts: One—Sound and Spelling; Two—Meaning and Spelling; Three—Rules and Spelling. Part One concentrates on the sound difficulties of the words themselves and on the problems of correct pronunciation and enunciation. Part Two emphasizes the words whose meaning determines both choice and spelling. Part Three stresses some simple rules for words ending in final e, final y, plurals, and the like. Although the word "rules" may set up an initial adverse reaction, the few given in this text will provide a basis for spelling a great number of words correctly.

Research has proven that good spellers have a method for spelling, and since that method is usually dividing words into parts, an appendix entitled Guidelines for Syllabication appears at the conclusion of the text. This concise presentation, stressing the simultaneous process of looking, hearing, and writing, will provide sufficient tools to divide not only the words in the text but also words encountered in the future.

The text is not a panacea for all spelling ills, but for those who misspell words like *beginning, desirous, definite, loneliness,* and many others, it offers concrete help to overcome these difficulties. It also furnishes a solid basis for independent study by making the student aware that pronunciation and sound, etymology and sound, meaning, and syllabication play important parts in good spelling.

It is hoped that the etymological references throughout will stimulate the curiosity of those who read the text and motivate them to study further the origins of the English language and the role they play in spelling and meaning.

TO THE STUDENT

1. *Plan of the text.* Each chapter and Appendix A have a pretest and posttest. The pretest is a *diagnostic* device. If you have ninety percent of the answers correct, you may bypass the chapter and go on to the next. The posttest is a *progress* device. It shows you how much improvement you have made since the pretest. Since each chapter has several reviews, it is suggested that you delay taking the posttest(s). You could do this in a number of ways: (1) Wait one or two days or longer upon completion of a chapter; (2) complete several chapters and then take the corresponding posttests; (3) finish each part and then take the posttests.

Before you begin, read the introduction to Appendix A and take the pretest. Since syllabication is basic to the entire text, you must determine whether you need to read this part. Your score will indicate what you should do.

To give you immediate and complete references for any word(s) you misspell, there is a listing of answer numbers and the corresponding chapter frames after each pretest and posttest. Be sure to read the instructions for looking up your wrong answers, if you have any.

2. *Responding.* You are expected to read carefully and at times slowly, as one frame is dependent upon another for understanding by the student. In other words, you must work out and apply what you learn. Several types of frames require different responses, including filling in letters, writing of words or parts of words, discriminating between groups of words, writing answers of several phrases. Even though you can answer some frames quickly with just mental responses, it is better to write out your answers.

Each frame is numbered and may require more than one response. If dotted lines appear in a frame, write your answer(s) for questions up to those lines and check to see if you are correct—then go on to the next part of the same frame. If a frame requires more than one response and does *not* have dotted lines, answer *all* parts and then check. Because the answers are immediately available, it is possible to cheat. Since eyes that wander will not improve your spelling, cover the answer side of the page with a small card (a 3 by 5 will do), sliding it down as you check the answer(s) to one frame but not revealing those for the next frame.

If you have a wrong answer, reread the frame. Don't hesitate about going back over a frame or two—there is no penalty for rereading. If you miss a question or **two** (or parts of a question) in a review, return to the beginning of that particular unit or to the specific frames pertinent to the wrong answer, and refresh your memory. It may be necessary to reread only a few frames for a better start.

3. *Timing.* Each chapter is divided into units of material with a review for each unit. Since these units are fairly short, try to stop after a review so that a lapse of time will not interrupt your learning of related material or a specific concept.

Since this is programmed material, you may make your own schedule, working more rapidly or slowly as you wish or as the material demands.

Each frame is not the same length, so don't anticipate finishing the same number in each chapter in the same number of minutes. Some that call for discrimination and application will necessarily take longer than some that require the writing of a word.

If you do not know the meaning of a word in either the introductory or the explanatory material, consult the dictionary. Any time spent with the dictionary is worthwhile, and in this case it will increase your understanding of the text and your vocabulary as well.

SPELLING IMPROVEMENT
A PROGRAM FOR SELF-INSTRUCTION

Part One
SOUND
AND SPELLING

Chapter 1

PRONUNCIATION AND ENUNCIATION

Words can be misspelled because they are not pronounced correctly. Some are mispronounced, with syllables added or omitted; others are not enunciated clearly and distinctly. The words in this chapter have been selected not only for their frequency in being misspelled, but also for their usefulness in illustrating that faulty pronunciation can cause spelling problems. Since specific words comprise the material for you to work with, the objectives for the chapter will be directly concerned with them: to pronounce the words correctly, observing the troublesome spots; to master their spelling; to use them in and out of context; and to encourage you to pronounce and enunciate all words distinctly.

PRETEST

Complete the words below. The definitions will help you to identify them.

1. hin____ance   obstruction
2. rec____nize   acknowledge
3. ath_____   competitor in sports
4. misch_____ous   playful
5. light____ing   making lighter
6. trag_____   dramatic, disastrous event
7. chim_____   passage for smoke and gas
8. temper_____   degree of hotness and coldness
9. ath_____ics   competitive sports
10. li__ble   responsible for
11. fin____ly   last, at the end
12. dis____trous   calamitous

13. veg_____   edible plant

14. light_____   electrical discharge

15. prej_____   adverse judgment, bias

16. fed_____al   connected with central government

17. remem_____ance   reminder or token

18. griev_____   serious

19. temper_____   manner of behaving

20. quan_____ty   number or amount

21. gov_____ment   process of running political units

22. envi_____ment   surroundings

23. back_____   education, experience

24. gra_____tude   thankfulness

25. hun_____   100

26. ag_____vate   make worse

---

2 3

1. In the first group are words to which an extra syllable is often added. Take *athlete* and *athletics*. You will sometimes hear them pronounced this way: "ath a lete" or "ath a let ics." These are wrong, of course, as *athlete* has just _____ syllables and *athletics* only _____.

ath lete
ath let ics

2. Pronounce the syllables carefully, then write them here: _____ _____ and _____ _____ _____.

athlete
athletics

3. One who takes part in sports is an _____ and the name for competitive sports is _____.

2 3

4. Here is another pair: *grievous* and *mischievous*. Often they are pronounced with an extra syllable, but if you say them correctly—griev'ous mis'chievous—you will hear only _____ syllables in *grievous* and _____ in *mischievous*.

griev ous
mis chie vous

5. Pronounce them once more and complete the syllables: griev _____ and mis _____ _____.

mischievous
grievous

6. It was not a harmful prank, just a mis _____ one.
     The two brothers were responsible for the gr_____ deed.

mischievous
grievous

7. The _____ child did not commit a _____ sin.

3

8. The following words have a common problem. Because they can remind you of a related word, you may include a part of that related word. Take the adjective *disastrous*, which means calamitous. It can remind you of the noun *disaster*, and too often the third syllable (*ter*) is included in the spelling of the adjective "dis as ter ous." *Disastrous*, correctly pronounced and spelled, has how many syllables? _____

disastrous

9. The results of the election were disas_____.

disastrous

10. The epidemic of sleeping sickness produced _____ _____ results.

is not

11. Pronounce it once more. There (is, is not) a syllable that sounds like *ter* in this word. _____

2
hin drance

12. Like *disastrous*, the word *hindrance* must be pronounced correctly to be spelled correctly. It can remind you of the verb *hinder* (to obstruct), but this reminder can cause you to put an extra syllable in the noun, like "hin der ance." Now pronounce *hindrance*. It has just _____ syllables. What is the second syllable: hin _____.

hindrance

13. The verb *to hinder* means to obstruct; the noun meaning an obstruction is _____.

remember

14. The noun *remembrance* has the same problem. It can remind you of what verb? _____

no

15. Pronounce the two words carefully: *remember, remembrance*. Is there a syllable in the noun that sounds liks "ber"? _____

re mem brance

16. Divide the word into syllables: _____ _____ _____.

remembrance

17. My grandmother gave me her gold watch as a re _____.

3

18. *Remembrance* has only _____ syllables.

2

19. To be spelled accurately, two other words must also be pronounced correctly: *lightning* and *chimney*. Look at and then pronounce each. Both have _____ syllables.

2

20. Should you pronounce *lightning* with an extra syllable (like "light en ing") you will spell another word, *lightening*, which means becoming lighter. *Lightening* has three syllables. The word you want to spell, defined as an electrical discharge, has how many syllables? _____

lightning

21. Our electric power went out when _____

lightning, lightening

hit the transformer.

lightning

22. Sharp bolts of thunder accompanied the jagged streaks of _____.

chim ney

23. Like *lightning*, the word *chimney* must not have an added syllable. It is not a "chim i ney," but a _____.

chimney

24. The passage through which smoke and gases escape from a furnace is called a _____.

2

25. The key to spelling *chimney* and *lightning* is to pronounce only _____ syllables in each word.

REVIEW

a. grievous
b. lightning
c. athlete
d. hindrance
e. mischievous
f. remembrance
g. chimney
h. athletics
i. disastrous
j. lightening

26. Now test your skill and fill in the missing letters. The definitions for the words are at the right.

a. griev_____ serious

b. light_____ electrical discharge

c. ath_____ competitor in sports

d. hin_____ obstruction

e. mis_____ playful

f. re_____ reminder or token

g. chim_____ passage for smoke

h. ath_____ competitive sports

i. dis_____ calamitous

j. light_____ becoming lighter

second (the *a*)

27. The second set of words is also an exercise in pronunciation, but it differs from the first in that letters or syllables are omitted, not added. For example, take *liable*, meaning responsible for or likely. It is sometimes pronounced "li ble." But the word is *li a ble*. Which syllable is usually omitted? _____

3	**28.** The word has how many syllables? _____
liable	**29.** The word meaning responsible for or likely is _____.
liable	**30.** Who is _____ for the damages to the car?
second	**31.** Like *liable*, the word *federal* causes a problem because the _____ syllable is left out.
fed er al	**32.** Like *liable*, the word *federal* has three syllables. Pronounce this word, and then divide it: ____ ____ ____.
Federal	**33.** My uncle has a position with the Fed_____ Communications Commission.
federal	**34.** Nancy must decide between a job with the state or one with the _____ government.
third (the *a*) third (the *a*) second (the *e*)	**35.** Over the years different pronunciations of words have developed, and occasionally they can cause spelling problems. The words *temperature*, *temperament*, and *vegetable* are good examples. Pronounce each quickly. Each sounds as if it had only three syllables. Which syllable is usually omitted: temperature _____, temperament _____, vegetable _____.
vowel	**36.** In each case you have a syllable in the middle of the word that consists of a single (consonant, vowel). _____
a. temperature b. temperament c. vegetable	**37.** Now complete these sentences: a. The storm caused a severe drop in _____. b. My cousin Mary Ann has a nervous _____. c. I don't like a _____ with my meal.
t	**38.** The following group of words also has a common problem: if they are not pronounced clearly a letter, in this case a consonant, can be omitted. For example, each syllable in the noun *quantity* must be pronounced distinctly; otherwise what letter can you omit in the second syllable: quan ti ty? _____
ti	**39.** The second syllable consists of what two letters? _____
quantity	**40.** A number or amount of anything is called _____.
t	**41.** In the word that means number or amount, do not forget the consonant _____ in the second syllable.

l

finally

final   ly

n

ern

government

government

beginning

ron

environment

environment

g

42. The adverb *finally* has two parts: the root and the suffix: *final   ly.* When adding *ly* you keep the complete root, so there will be two _____'s in the word.

43. After six hours of debate, the legislature _____ came to an agreement.

44. The word that means at last or at the end consists of the root word _____ and the suffix _____.

45. Like *finally,* the word *government* has a consonant that must be pronounced distinctly; otherwise it may be omitted in the spelling. Pronounce the word by syllables: gov ern ment. Now say it quickly. What consonant in the second syllable can be passed over? _____

46. In other words, it is the second syllable that causes the misspelling: gov _____ ment.

47. My cousin worked sixteen years for the federal _____ _____.

48. The professor then asked, "What form of _____ _____ would be best in this case?"

49. *Environment* has a slightly different problem, but again it is the pronunciation that causes the difficulty. Pronounce the word by syllables: en vi ron ment. Unlike *government* (where the problem is at the end of the second syllable) *environment* has the difficulty at the _____ of the third syllable.

50. Spell this important third syllable: en vi _____ ment.

51. If pollution is not checked in the near future, our _____ will be ruined.

52. An individual can be affected greatly by his _____ _____.

53. The word *background* consists of two words, and although usage has combined them into solid form, both retain their entities as complete words: *back   ground.* Pronunciation again enters the picture because careless pronunciation can cause misspelling. The consonant that is often left out is _____.

ground
background

54. The space behind closer areas is called back_____.
Thus in paintings the space farther back which provides
relief for the principal objects portrayed is the _____
_____.

background

55. A person's experience and training can also be called
_____.

REVIEW

a. *11*
b. *a*
c. *a*
d. *er*
e. *ti*
f. *a*
g. *ern*
h. *g*
i. *ron*
j. *e*

56. Fill in the missing letter(s).

a. fina_____y   f. temper___ture

b. li___ble   g. gov_____ment

c. temper___ment   h. back___round

d. fed_____al   i. envi_____ment

e. quan_____ty   j. veg___table

a. environment
b. vegetable
c. liable
d. quantity
e. temperature
f. government
g. federal
h. finally
i. background
j. temperament

57. Complete the words matching these definitions.

a. surroundings   en_____

b. edible plant   veg_____

c. responsible   li_____

d. number   qu_____

e. heat or cold   tem_____

f. process of   gov_____
   ruling

g. referring to   fed_____
   central ruling

h. lastly   fi_____

i. space behind   back_____

j. manner of behaving tem_____

t

58. Mispronunciation also causes misspelling of the last
set of words. Take the noun *gratitude*. Pronouncing the
word carefully will produce a correctly spelled word:
grat i tude, not grad i tude. Which consonant in
the first syllable causes the difficulty? _____

grat i tude

59. Complete the first two syllables: _____ _____
tude.

gratitude

60. The noun which means thankfulness is _____.

gratitude	**61.** For his kindness and generosity I expressed my deep _____ .
a	**62.** Now pronounce *hundred* by syllables: hun dred. Which combination is at the beginning of the second syllable: (a) two consonants, or (b) a consonant and a vowel? _____
dr	**63.** Here you have the problem: *hun dred*, not hun derd. What consonants must precede the e? _____
hundred	**64.** The figure 100 stands for the word _____ .
hundred	**65.** There were about a _____ people at the meeting.
second	**66.** The word *aggravate* is similar to *hundred* in that two consonants must precede the vowel to prevent the mis-spelling of the word. Pronounce it carefully: ag gra vate. Which syllable will cause the problem? _____
gr	**67.** In the second syllable what two consonants precede the vowel *a*? _____
aggravate	**68.** To make worse or make more of a trouble is the meaning of ag_____ .
aggravate	**69.** In informal writing, to annoy or to vex can also be the meaning of _____ .
og	**70.** If not correctly pronounced, the second syllable of *recognize* can cause trouble. Through carelessness it is easy to omit which letters? rec_____nize
rec og nize	**71.** Write the three syllables of this word: _____ _____ _____ .
recognize	**72.** If we acknowledge someone on the street we rec _____ him.
recognize	**73.** Only after careful study will I _____ the validity of your argument.
a. 3 b. trag prej c. vowel d. trag e dy prej u dice	**74.** The last two words take careful pronunciation and distinction of syllables: *tragedy* and *prejudice*. Pronounce them slowly, then answer these questions: a. How many syllables does each have? _____ b. Each has only four letters in the first syllable: _____ and _____ .

c. Each has a single (vowel, consonant) in the second syllable. _____

d. Now syllabify each word:
_____ _____ _____ and _____ _____ _____.

tragedy

75. A dramatic, disastrous event is called a tr_____.

tragedy

76. The terrible earthquake in Peru is a great _____.

prejudice

77. An adverse opinion or judgment made without sufficient knowledge is known as prej_____.

prejudice

78. Mr. Doe has allowed his life to be ruled by _____
_____.

REVIEW

a. aggravate
b. hundred
c. recognize
d. prejudice
e. gratitude
f. tragedy

79. Supply the correct words for these definitions.

a. To make worse is the meaning of _____.

b. The figure 100 can be written like this: _____.

c. If you acknowledge a friend's fault, you _____ it.

d. Adverse judgment is called _____.

e. Thankfulness is the meaning of _____.

f. A dramatic, disastrous event is a _____.

POSTTEST

Every word you have studied in this chapter is included in the following sentences. Read each sentence carefully and from the context and meaning clue supply the missing words.

1. Last July the _____ soared into the 100s.

2. Stan is a fine _____.
          competitor in sports

3. It is a gr_____ matter.

4. Can you apply for a position with the _____ government?
      central

5. I would like the necklace as a _____.
     reminder

6. Tad will not eat a _____ with his meal.

7. People are affected by both heredity and _____.
      surroundings

8. Black smoke poured from the _____.
     passage

9. Do you have a sufficient _____ of tax forms?
      amount

10. When will you be _____
responsible
for paying your own debts?

11. Lucy has a nervous _____.

12. There were about a _____
100
people present.

13. The new laws will only _____
make worse
the situation.

14. Far too much _____
bias
exists today.

15. Did he _____
acknowledge
you when he passed you?

16. The transformer was struck by
_____.

17. The earthquake was _____.
calamitous

18. The red-haired girl is very _____.
playful

19. The boy next door takes part in
_____.
sports

20. The sky is gradually _____
becoming lighter
_____.

21. His going will be a _____.
obstruction

22. To play the hero's role well, Don
needs a good dramatic back_____.

23. Shakespeare's *Hamlet* is considered a great _____.

24. He ended his speech _____.
at last

25. The newly formed nation has what
kind of _____?
political process

26. The young boy expressed his
_____.
thankfulness

Chapter 2

PREFIXES

Confusing one prefix with another is easy to do, but it is just as easy to learn not to. How? By becoming aware of the part that pronunciation and meaning play in adding prefixes to the beginning of words, you can overcome any prefix difficulties quickly and surely.

The objectives of this chapter are four: you will pronounce carefully words that include prefixes, like *per-pre-pro* and *dis-de;* you will write the correct meaning for these and other troublesome prefixes; you will choose the correct prefix for particular root words; and you will write correctly a number of commonly misspelled words. Upon attaining these objectives, you will be better equipped to select the correct prefix for other words, familiar and unfamiliar.

PRETEST

A. Choose the correct spelling for each definition.

1. to scatter   disseminate, diseminate _____

2. to spell incorrectly   mispell, misspell _____

3. not required   unnecessary, unecessary _____

4. to recall   reccollect, recollect _____

5. to differ   disent, dissent _____

6. an error   misstake, mistake _____

7. to cut up   disect, dissect _____

8. artificial   unnatural, unatural _____

9. to advise   recommend, reccommend _____

B. Choose the correct prefix for each root word. Meanings are given to help you identify the words.

10. _____form   to act
    pre, per

11. _____pare   to get ready
    per, pre, pro

12. _____satisfied   not pleased
    dis, de

13. _____ceed   to go ahead
    pre, pro, per

14. _____cede   to go before
    per, pro, pre

15. _____cide   come to a conclusion
    dis, de

16. _____scribe   denounce or condemn
    pre, per, pro

17. _____scribe   tell about something
    dis, de

18. _____scribe   set down as a rule
    pre, pro, per

a. *dis*
b. *de*
c. *de*
d. *dis*
e. *de*
f. *dis*
g. *de*

1. In certain words the prefixes *dis* and *de* have so similar a pronunciation that it is easy to substitute one for the other. For example, the sound of *i* in *dismiss* is the short sound. The sound of e in *describe* is also the short sound of *i*; and since s follows the e in describe you have the basis for confusion: "dis   cribe." The solution lies in the meaning of the prefixes. For instance, *dis* means apart. If one is dismissed, he is sent apart. The prefix also means not. To dislike someone is not to like him. The prefix de has two meanings. First, it means down. If you descend, you go down. Second, it means off (or away). To deduct a dollar is to take it off (or away).

Consider the meanings of *dis* and *de* and choose the correct prefix for each root or base below. For bases not easily identified the meanings are given.

a. _____approve   e. _____tour   (turn)

b. _____tain   (hold)   f. _____tend   (stretch)

c. _____part   (go)   g. _____cay   (fall)

d. _____trust

a. apart
b. off
c. down
d. not

2. Now write the correct meaning for each underlined prefix.

a. If you *dissect* a frog, you cut it _____.

b. If you *decide*, you cut _____ deliberation.

c. If you *degrade* something, you grade it _____.

d. If you *distrust* someone, you do _____ have confidence in him.

a. not apart
b. down off (away)

3. Supply two meanings for each prefix.

a. *dis* _____   _____

b. *de* _____   _____

a. dis
b. de
c. dis
d. de
e. dis
f. de

4. Read these sentences carefully for their meaning, then supply the missing prefix, *dis* or *de*.

a. His actions _____ honored the family name.

b. The mountaineers had difficulty trying to _____scend.

c. The supervisor's easygoing manner _____pelled her fears.

d. You should rewrite your _____scription.

e. There is always a place in society for constructive _____sent.

f. After a while she became _____spondent.

a. through
b. forward or forth
c. before

5. Confusing the prefixes *pre, per,* and *pro* usually results from similarities in pronunciation, from not knowing their meanings, and from not looking at them carefully. Since *you* can look at and pronounce these elements correctly, we are concerned here with their meanings:

pre before
pro forward or forth
per through

For the following sentences write the correct meaning of each prefix.

a. A performer is one who carries his act _____.

b. A proposal is a plan that is brought _____.

c. To precede is to go _____.

a. per
b. pre
c. pro
d. per

6. Now supply the correct missing prefix.

a. If you act or carry through you will _____form.

b. If you go before me you will _____cede me.

c. To place an idea forward is to _____pose it.

d. To see all the way through is to _____ceive it.

pre before
pro forward (forth)
per through

7. Write these three prefixes and their meanings.

_____ means _____
_____ means _____
_____ means _____

a. per through
b. pre before

8. Read each sentence, then supply the correct prefix (*per-pre-pro*) and its meaning for each of these definitions.

c. *pro* forth
d. *per* through
e. *pro* forward
f. *pre* before

a. To _____meate is to soak _____.

b. To _____cede is to go _____.

c. To _____claim is to cry _____.

d. To _____forate is to punch holes _____
something.

e. A _____cession is a movement of people going

_____.

f. To _____cancel is to cancel a postage stamp _____
mailing.

REVIEW

a. pre
b. per
c. de
d. de
e. de
f. de
g. dis
h. per per pro
i. pro
j. pro
k. through
l. forward
m. before

9. Test your skill in choosing the correct prefixes or their meanings.

a. When my cousin had a severe reaction to the new drug, the doctor said he would _____scribe another
per, pre
drug.

b. To sweat or excrete a fluid through the pores of the skin is to _____spire.
pre, per

c. How many times must I _____scribe her dress?
dis, de

d. A severe earthquake will _____stroy even the well-
dis, de
constructed buildings.

e. The father of the little boy is filled with grief and _____spair.
de, dis

f. Senator Fowler stated that he could easily _____spise
dis, de
all dishonest businessmen.

g. The constant drumming of his fingertips on the table will surely _____turb the patients.
de, dis

h. The instructor _____forms duties _____taining to
pre, per   per, pre
his _____fession.
per, pre, pro

i. Even though I missed a month of school, the teachers decided to _____mote me.
pre, pro

j. The high schools need a different _____cedure for registration.
pro, pre

k. Perform means to act _____.
   through, before

l. To propose is to place _____.
   before, forward

m. To precede is to go _____.
   through, before

a. apart   not
b. down   off (away)

10. Supply the meanings for these prefixes:

a. *dis*   _____ or _____

b. *de*   _____ or _____

again   back

11. The prefix *re* can mean again or back. For instance, to reenter is to enter _____; to recall some information is to call it _____.

back   again

12. Two commonly misspelled words are *recommend* and *recollect*. Each contains the prefix *re* and a root word. If one recollects he recalls or collects _____; if he recommends he commends _____.

collect   commend

13. These two words have the prefix *re* and a root word. What are the roots? _____ and _____.

recommends
recollect

14. If an employer says an employee is worthy of a promotion, he _____ him.
   I find it hard to _____ the exact details of the accident.

a. again
b. back
c. back
d. again

15. Now supply the correct meaning of *re* in each word below.

a. request: to seek _____

b. recall: to call _____

c. a reprieve: a taking _____

d. a reprint: a printing _____

a. misstep
b. disservice
c. unnumbered
d. mistake
e. misstate
f. unnerved
g. mistreat
h. uncertainty
i. disrepair
j. dissolve

16. Most of the spelling problems with the prefixes *mis*, *dis*, and *un* come from forgetting that the prefix and the root are two entities. For example, *mis* ends in s and *spell* begins with s. When you combine them, you must keep both s's. The same is true when you add *un* to a word beginning with *n*. With this in mind, add the specified prefixes and the roots below.

a. mis   step   _____

b. dis   service   _____

c. un numbered _____

d. mis take _____

e. mis state _____

f. un nerved _____

g. mis treat _____

h. un certainty _____

i. dis repair _____

j. dis solve _____

REVIEW

a. recommend
b. recollect (or recall)
c. recommendation
d. unnatural
e. misspelled
f. unnecessary
g. dissatisfied
h. misstated
i. mistakes

17. Read each sentence carefully, then write the required word.

a. To commend again is to _____.

b. To call back some information is to _____ it.

c. Because of his poor work record, I cannot give him a _____ation.

d. His behavior is _____.
    un natural

e. Why are so many words _____?
    mis spelled

f. Your explanation is _____.
    un necessary

g. After using the new product for a month I am _____.
    dis satisfied

h. He has _____ the facts.
    mis stated

i. She makes far too many _____ in typing.
    mis takes

POSTTEST

Choose the correct prefix and write the whole word.

1. To sweat means to _____spire.
   pro, per, pre

2. I asked the doctor for a new _____scription.
   pro, pre, de

3. Mr. Roe finally _____suaded her
   pre, per
   to leave.

4. He felt nothing but absolute _____
   dis, de
   spair.

5. To set above in favor is the meaning of _____fer.
   pro, pre

6. In ten minutes the black ink _____meated the rug.
   per, pro, pre

7. Can you _____scribe the sunset?
   dis, de

8. Before I finished my rebuttal of the first point, I was ordered to _____ceed to the next.
   pre, pro, per

9. I could not _____sect the frog.
   de, dis

10. The doctor granted his _____
    pre, per
    mission to go home.

Supply the prefix meaning for each sentence.

11. In destroying you are tearing _____.

12. Permanent means changeless, or remaining _____out.

13. A distraction is something that draws you _____.

14. To recall is to call _____.

15. The state of being perplexed is to be literally "entwined" all the way _____.

16. To disserve is to treat badly, or _____ to serve one.

17. If you desist, you abstain from doing something, or you stand _____ _____.

18. When you precede another, you go _____ him.

19. A person's decease (or death) is his going _____.

20. If someone is disreputable he is _____ reputable.

Chapter 3

SYLLABICATION

Although etymology and pronunciation can be helpful in spelling words correctly, syllabication can be the answer for particularly troublesome words. To divide words into syllables you need to know about vowels, semivowels, dipthongs, consonants, long and short sounds of vowels, and major and minor stress. If you are not familiar with all this, or if you need a refresher, work through Appendix A before you begin this chapter. If you need only the guidelines begin with frame 13 of the appendix. Since the material in this chapter is predicated on your knowing how to syllabify words, it might be worth your while to work the entire appendix anyway. At any rate the pretest to the appendix can tell you immediately whether you should or should not.

In this chapter you will (1) learn a five-step method of spelling words through syllabication; (2) use this method in spelling specific words; (3) recognize what elements in words to look and listen for; (4) spell a number of words in and out of context; and (5) reproduce these words from definition clues. It is hoped that you will use this reliable method in spelling unfamiliar and other familiar but bothersome words.

PRETEST

Fill in the missing letters. Meanings are given to help you identify the words.

1. in_____est   concern, curiosity
2. embar_____   make ill at ease
3. irrel__vant   not related
4. ser_____   noncommissioned rank in Army
5. vil_____   scoundrel

6. expe_____   knowledge, skill
7. ac_____   get possession of
8. im_____ately   right now
9. dis_____faction   displeasure
10. vac_____   cleaning appliance
11. ap_____ent   readily seen or understood
12. con_____ience   comfort
13. pro_____dure   method of proceeding
14. oc_____ally   from time to time
15. disap_____   not come up to expectations
16. lon_____ness   dejection and sadness
17. op_____nity   occasion
18. fin_____cier   expert in finance
19. discrim_____ation   prejudice
20. par_____el   going same direction
21. ac_____late   amass, gather
22. disap_____   vanish
23. inter_____   break between
24. res_____   eating place
25. ap_____ciate   recognize, become aware of
26. ac_____ance   someone you know slightly
27. ex_____ation   act of explaining
28. ac_____plishment   act of succeeding
29. pos_____sion   ownership

1. Several words have what is called the "double conso-nant" difficulty: sometimes an extra consonant is added, other times a consonant is omitted. We shall eliminate the problem by establishing a procedure for dividing words into syllables.

(1) Look at the word carefully (look for familiar roots, prefixes, suffixes, silent letters, double letters, and the like).

(2) Say the word distinctly and correctly. If you are not sure about the pronunciation, check the dictionary. Look for pronounced vowels as a guide to the number of syllables.

a. both
yes
• • • • • • • • • • • • •
b. 4
4
short
• • • • • • • • • • • • •
c. ac com plish
    ment
d. accomplishment
• • • • • • • • • • • • •
e. accomplishment

(3) Sound the word in syllables and then write it.

(4) Write the word from memory and check for the correct spelling.

(5) Use it in sentences. Be sure you know what the word means.

a. Now take the word *accomplishment*. Look at it carefully. Do you find a prefix or a suffix or both? _____ Do you find a double consonant? _____
• •
b. Now pronounce it. How many pronounced vowels does it have? _____ How many syllables are there? _____ Does the second syllable have a short or long sound of o?

_____

• •
c. Mentally sound the word as you write it in syllables:

_____ _____ _____ _____ .

d. Write it quickly from memory:

_____ .

• •
e. Use it in one or more sentences. The professor told me that my reaching the quota was quite an _____

_____ .

look
say (pronounce)
in syllables
in sentences

2. To review the procedure: you first _____ at the word carefully, then _____ it distinctly, sound out and write the word (as a whole, in syllables) write it from memory and check the spelling, and finally use it (in phrases, in sentences) _____

4
ac cu mu late

3. Here is the second word *accumulate*, which means to amass or gather. Perform the first two steps on your own. How many syllables are there? _____ What are they?

_____

accumulate

4. Write the word from memory: _____ .

a. accumulate
b. accumulate

5. Now use it in context:

a. Jane's father exclaimed, "How many books did you _____ in a year!"

b. This house can _____ more dust than any other I've known.

ap pre ci ate

6. The next four words also have a double consonant difficulty. The first is *appreciate*. In mastering the spelling of this word, you first look at it carefully, pronounce it distinctly, and then divide it into syllables: _____

_____ .

appreciate

7. The word which means to estimate the value of something or to fully realize a situation is _____.

appreciate
appreciated

8. Even though I haven't been poverty-stricken, I think I can _____ the dire problems involved.
               realize
The professor _____ the efforts of
                           valued
his students.

3 *p*
• • • • • • • • • • • •
ap par ent
apparent

9. On your own perform the first two steps with the word *apparent*. It has _____ syllables and a double consonant _____ near the beginning of the word.
• •
Perform the third step: _____.
And now the fourth: _____.

apparent
apparent
apparent

10. To be readily understood is the definition of the word

_____.
That he has a mastery of his subject is _____.
Are my feelings about religion that _____?

c
oc ca sion al ly

11. Look carefully at the adverb *occasionally*. It has only one s but it has two _____'s.
Now divide it into syllables: _____.

occasionally
occasionally
occasionally

12. Write it quickly from memory: _____.
Now use it in these sentences:
I go to the theater _____.
Will you accompany me _____ to the symphony concerts?

op por tu ni ty

13. Here is the word *opportunity*. Look at it . . . pronounce it . . . and remembering the guidelines for a long and short vowel, divide it into syllables: _____

_____.

a. opportunity
b. opportunity

14. Combine the fourth and fifth steps:

a. The noun that means a suitable occasion or time is

_____.

b. Will we ever have an _____ to meet the famous pitcher?

occasional*ly*

15. Fill in the missing letters: oc___asional_____.

REVIEW

16. From the meaning clues supply the appropriate words you have just studied.

a. The verb meaning to amass is _____.

b. We used to drive to the ranch every Sunday; now we go only _____.

c. No matter what the outcome is, I do _____
                                                    value
your efforts to promote the campaign.

d. After reviewing Jim's work in art history, the instructor said, "That's quite an _____!"
                                        successful completion

e. I've never had the _____ to attend
                                        occasion
a rock festival.

f. She made her intentions quite _____.
                                        readily understood

a. accumulate
b. occasionally
c. appreciate
d. accomplishment
e. opportunity
f. apparent

first
4
dis sat is fac tion

17. Here are four words with the same beginning, the prefix *dis.* Remember that a prefix is a separate unit, so the addition of a prefix usually does not disturb the word or the prefix. The noun *dissatisfaction* is simply the combination of *satisfaction* and *dis* (meaning not), so the whole word means a state of not being satisfied, or displeasure. Look at the word carefully and then pronounce it.
Which syllable is the prefix? _____
How many other syllables are there? _____
Write the word in syllables: _____.

a. dissatisfaction
b. dissatisfaction

18. Use the word in these contexts:

a. To have a feeling of displeasure is to have one of
_____.

b. Mr. Brown registered his _____
by shouting at the chairman.

dissatisfaction

19. The new wage proposals caused the most _____
_____ among the lowest paid drivers.

prefix
crim i na tion

20. Perform the first two steps for this word: *discrimination. Dis* is a (prefix, suffix) _____. Now divide the rest of the word into syllables, watching your vowel sounds: _____.

discrimination

21. This word has two common meanings. The first is an act of prejudice: There is too much _____ between the races and sexes.

discrimination

22. Another meaning is the ability to see fine distinctions: In his reviews of operatic performances, Mr. Bucher shows a keen _____ .

dis   p

23. *Disappoint* and *disappear* have two similarities: both have the prefix _____ and both have a double _____ in the root.

dis ap point
dis ap pear

24. Now pronounce the words and separate each into syllables: _____
_____

a. disappear
b. disappoint
c. disappoint
d. disappear

25. Read these sentences and write the correct one of these two for each.

a. Perhaps I can catch them before they _____ from sight.

b. If you don't go with me, you will _____ me.

c. When students do not work hard, they often _____
_____ their teachers.

d. In time the trumpeter swan may _____ .

im me di ate ly

26. The next group of words also has double consonant difficulties. The first is *immediately*. Perform the first two steps . . . now divide it into syllables: _____
_____ .

immediately

27. To respond without hesitation or delay is to answer
_____ .

immediately

28. The children were trained to reply _____ .

3
s

29. The second word in this group is *possession*. Look . . . pronounce . . . how many syllables does the word have? ___ There are two sets of ___'s.

pos ses sion

30. Now divide it:_____ .

possessions

31. A few clothes and a toothbrush comprise his worldly
_____ .

possession

32. There is an old saying that _____
ownership
is nine-tenths of the law.

yes
l
par al lel

second   third

ll

parallel

em bar rass

embarrass

embarrass

a. dissatisfaction
b. disappear
c. parallel
d. possession
e. discrimination
f. immediately
g. embarrass
h. disappoint

33. Perform the initial steps for this word: *parallel.*
Does it have a double letter? _____
What is it? _____
What are the syllables? _____

34. One of the double letters completes the _____ syllable and the second begins the _____ syllable.

35. The two *l*'s standing so nicely together match the geometric definition of the word: two (or more) straight lines that do not intersect. Look for the straight lines in para____el.

36. This word also means having comparable parts: The construction of the two sentences is _____.

37. The word *embarrass* can best be spelled correctly by dividing it into syllables. But first look at it . . . then pronounce it . . . and now divide it: _____.

38. To cause someone to be ill at ease or to hamper with financial difficulties are definitions of the word _____
_____.

39. Jack's intention was to _____ his sister.

REVIEW

40. From the clues presented in each sentence, write the correct word for each.

a. Reverend Dunn showed his _____
                                    displeasure
with the program by closing the hall.

b. The minute I suggest their doing the dishes, they
_____.
        vanish

c. Your red dots are not _____.
                            comparable

d. How many appliances do you have in your pos_____
_____?

e. Now there are laws against _____.
                                prejudice

f. May I return the book tomorrow or do you want it
_____?
        right now

g. I was afraid to tell her because I might _____

<u>put ill at ease</u>

her.

h. I surely hope Mrs. Brown doesn't _____

<u>fail to meet expectations</u>

me.

first
1 2
ac quire
ac quain tance

41. Two words often misspelled have the same beginning: *acquire* and *acquaintance*. The misspelling is caused partly by poor pronunciation and partly by not studying the word. Perform the first two steps on your own.
Since *ac* is the prefix it is the _____ syllable in each word.
How many syllables are left in acquire? _____ in acquaintance? _____
Now syllabify the two words: _____ and

_____.

acquire

42. If Mr. Hancock wants to get possession of 10 percent of his company's stock, he wants to _____ it.

acquaintance

43. A person you know less intimately than a friend is called an _____.

a. acquire
b. acquaintance
c. acquaintances
d. acquire

44. Write the correct word of these two in the following sentences.

a. Randy wants to _____ two lakeshore lots.

b. Jack is not a friend; he is only an _____.

c. Most people have quite a few _____.

d. Tom has worked hard to _____ all his trophies.

prefix (or *ir*)
3
(ir) rel e vant

45. Perform the first two steps for *irrelevant* (*ir* is a variant of the prefix *in*, meaning not).
What constitutes the first syllable? _____
How many more syllables are there? _____
What are they? _____

irrelevant

46. Write the word from memory: _____.

irrelevant

47. That which has no bearing on a particular case is

_____.

irrelevant

48. The teacher commented that some of my evidence was _____.

2
1
r
in ter rupt

49. The word *interrupt* is derived from the Latin *inter,* meaning between, and *rumpere,* to break. Look at and pronounce the word carefully.
How many syllables does the prefix have? _____
How many remaining syllables are there? _____
What letter ends the prefix and also begins the root? _____
Write the syllables: _____ .

interrupt

50. The word meaning to stop or break the continuity of is _____ .

interrupt

51. If you "break between" two persons carrying on a conversation, you will _____ them.

interrupt irrelevant

52. The chairman threatened to _____ the delegate's speech if some of his points were _____ .
                                                                          not related

3
3
e in first syllable
yes—suffix (ness)

53. The word *loneliness* presents no real problem so long as you look at it and pronounce it carefully.
How many pronounced vowels does it have? _____
How many syllables are there? _____
What vowel is not pronounced? _____
Are there added elements (prefix or suffix)? _____

lone li ness

54. Now for the syllables: _____ .

loneliness

55. If one is dejected, perhaps a bit sad, he is lonely; the state of being dejected is called _____ .

loneliness

56. Although surrounded by many friends, Sam lives a life of _____ .

ex pla na tion
pro ce dure

57. The spelling of these next words depends on your pronunciation of them and on your looking at them closely. Take *explanation* first and perform the first two steps. Then do the same for *procedure.* If you have done your work carefully, you can now divide them easily: _____
_____   _____ .

explanation
procedure

58. Write both words from memory: _____
_____ .

ex *pla* nation
pro ce dure

59. Notice that the last syllable of the verb *explain* is not spelled like the second syllable of the related noun: ex_____nation. Neither is the last syllable of *proceed* spelled like the second syllable of its related noun: pro_____dure.

explanation
procedure

60. To explain a point is to offer an _____;
a manner of proceeding is called a _____.

a. explanation
b. procedure
c. explanation
   procedure

61. Choose one or the other of these two words to fit the sentences below.

a. I doubt if he can give me a good _____.

b. I wonder what _____ he will initiate.

c. The noun that relates to explain is _____;
the one that relates to proceed is _____.

REVIEW

a. irrelevant
b. acquaintance
c. loneliness
d. procedure
e. acquire
f. explanation
g. procedure

62. From the contexts, write the appropriate words.

a. If a point is not related, it is _____.

b. Someone you know slightly can be called an _____
_____.

c. The doctor cannot rouse him from his state of _____
_____.
          dejection

d. What will be the _____ at the convention?
                  method

e. How long will it take to _____ the property?
                         possess

f. He gave a lengthy _____ of the new law.

g. Are you sure this is the right _____?

4
ex
ence

63. The word *experience* can present a problem, but only momentarily. First look at it, then pronounce it.
How many syllables has it? _____
What is the prefix? _____
What is the suffix? _____

e

64. We have the first and last syllables—now to divide to make the second and third: ex peri ence. Pronounce it again. Although the first vowel does not have a long sound as the *r* colors it, it is closer to this sound than to the short sound of e. Therefore, to get the second syllable you would divide after which letter? _____

ex pe ri ence

65. Now divide the whole word: _____.

experience

66. An event lived through is the definition of the word _____.

experience

67. A person can also _____ a feeling of loneliness.

3
ex
ience
vẹn

68. Although the last part of the word *convenience* is similar to *experience*, it is not pronounced the same. The last syllable (*ience*) has the sound of "yens." With this difference in mind, perform steps (1) and (2).
How many syllables are there? _____
The first syllable is the prefix _____.
The last syllable is _____.
The middle syllable is _____.

con ven ience

69. Now write the three syllables: _____.

convenience

70. A personal comfort, or something that increases comfort, like a toaster or fry pan, is a _____.

convenience

71. Will you ask the manager if I may see him at his _____?

2
first *l*
vil lain

72. Look at and pronounce this word: *villain.*
How many syllables are there? _____
Where do you divide after the first? _____
Divide the word into syllables: _____.

villain

73. A scoundrel can be called a _____.

villain

74. In a melodrama the character usually hissed at and booed by the audience is the _____.

3

75. *Interest* can be pronounced correctly with two or three syllables. But the spelling always has how many syllables? _____

interest

76. To hold the attention of a person is to in_____ him.

interest

77. A feeling of curiosity or fascination is the definition of the noun _____.

vac u um

78. Like *interest*, the word *vacuum* can be pronounced in two or three syllables, but to spell it correctly you must divide it graphically into three parts. Apply your guidelines and divide this word: _____.

vacuum vacuum

79. A space empty of matter is called a vac_____. A feeling of emptiness can be known as a _____.

vacuum

80. The electric appliance to clean rugs is also called a

_____.

res
tau rant

81. Two words, derived from Old French, have retained the spelling characteristics of the French language. The first is *restaurant*. If you remember the guideline about two consonants between two vowels, you can form the first syllable easily. What is the first syllable? _____.
The rest of the word falls naturally into two syllables:

_____ _____.

restaurant

82. An eating place is called a _____.

fin
an cier

83. The second word that has retained the French spelling is *financier*, an expert in financial affairs. The short vowel at the beginning gives the clue to the first syllable:

_____.

The rest of the word is easy to divide: _____.

financier

84. An expert in large-scale money affairs is known as a

_____.

financier

85. J. P. Morgan was a famous American _____.

3
is not
2
vowel is the same—
sergeant, servire

86. *Sergeant* also has a French "flavor" as its derivation goes back to Old French; however, its basic origin is the Latin verb *servire*, to serve. Since pronunciation alone will not give you the necessary clues to correct spelling, observe it closely.
How many vowels does it have? _____
The *a* in the second syllable (is, is not) pronounced?
So there are how many syllables? _____
What is the relationship of the first vowel in *sergeant* to the original Latin verb? _____

ser geant

87. Now divide the word: _____.

sergeant

88. One of the noncommissioned officer ranks in the Army is that of _____.

REVIEW

a. experience
b. villain
c. interest
d. convenience
e. sergeant
f. restaurant

89. From the clues given below write the correct word for each sentence.

a. John could not get the teaching position because he lacked ex_____.

b. The role I like to portray best is the _____.

g. financier
h. vacuum

c. I don't have any in_____ in collecting stamps.

d. Living a block from the store is a _____.
comfort

e. Lance was promoted to s_____.

f. Dining at a _____ is expensive.

g. An expert in financial affairs is a _____.

h. My niece bought a new _____.
rug cleaner

POSTTEST

Write the complete word. The beginnings of each word and the meaning are given to help you identify them.

1. vac_____ cleaning appliance
2. vil_____ scoundrel
3. in_____ concern
4. s_____ noncommissioned officer rank
5. em_____ make ill at ease
6. ac_____ get possession of
7. dis_____ vanish
8. ex_____ knowledge, skill
9. im_____ this minute
10. pro_____ method of proceeding
11. oc_____ now and then
12. lo_____ state of dejection
13. fin_____ financial expert
14. ap_____ readily seen
15. dis_____ prejudice
16. ac_____ amass, gather
17. op_____ occasion
18. con_____ comfort
19. inter_____ break between
20. ac_____ person slightly known
21. dis_____ displeasure
22. res_____ eating place

23. ap_____   be aware of
24. dis_____   fail to come up to expectation
25. ex_____   act of explaining
26. ac_____ment   act of succeeding
27. par_____   same direction, similar
28. pos_____   ownership
29. ir_____   not related

Chapter 4

SILENT LETTERS

If you have had words marked off because you left out a letter that was not sounded, usually called a silent letter, you may have wondered why the letter was there in the first place. In the Middle English period (the twelfth through the fifteenth centuries), some of the final e's and all the consonants were pronounced. For example, the *k* and *gh* in *knight* and the *k* in *know* were sounded. Many words from the Greek had initial letters sounded, like the *p* in *psychology* and *pneumonia.* Gradually the pronunciation of many words changed, some letters becoming silent. The fact that they are still silent does not mean that they are to be omitted. On the contrary, they are there to stay until such time as the spelling is changed. In this chapter, then, you will (1) recognize the relationship between the derivation and the present word; (2) practice spelling a number of useful words in and out of context; and (3) reproduce the words from given definitions. Remember that the meaning and the spelling of words are both important.

PRETEST

Fill in the missing letters. The definitions given will help you to identify the words.

1. W_____nesday   a day of the week
2. d_____t   something owed
3. con_____   criticize severely
4. g_____ian   one who protects
5. _____ology   study of the mind
6. r_____thm   recurring motion, measure
7. _____ledge   learning

8. und_____edly   beyond hesitation

9. ex_____st   to tire or wear out

10. g_____   to protect

11. s____tle   clever

12. ___riter   one who composes

13. _____iatry   medical treatment of the mind

14. dou__t   hesitate or waver

---

debt
doubt
undoubtedly
subtle

1. Four useful words have the same silent letter, having been derived from these Latin words: *debere,* meaning to owe; *dubitare,* meaning to waver; and *subtilis,* meaning thin and fine.
If you owe something you have a de__t.
If you hesitate or waver, you dou__t; if there is no wavering, you will undou__tedly succeed.
If you can make fine distinctions, or are clever, you are su__tle.

a. debt
b. doubt
c. undoubtedly
d. subtle

2. According to the context, write or complete these same four words.

a. When you haven't paid a bill, you still have a _____.

b. If you are in _____, do nothing.

c. The word that means accepted without doubt is un_____.

d. If one can make a point so "fine" as to be elusive or abstruse, he is said to be _____tle.

a. subtle
b. doubt
c. undoubtedly
d. debts

3. Now fit these four words into these contexts.

a. She has a reputation for being _____.

b. Why must he _____ everything I say?

c. He is _____ the most stubborn person I know.

d. Alex filed for bankruptcy because he had so many _____.

d

4. The word *Wednesday* comes from the Old English *Wodnesdaeg,* or "Woden's Day." Woden, as you may remember, was the chief Teutonic god, and since Wednesday relates directly to this proper name, it is right that the first syllable end in ____.

Woden's

5. You can best remember the silent letter in this word by recalling _____ Day.

Wednesday

6. The day after Tuesday is _____nesday.

Wednesday

7. This year Valentine's Day comes on _____.

h

8. Now pronounce the words *exhaust* and *rhythm* carefully. Which letter is not sounded? _____

does

9. The words are derived from the Latin *exhaurire* and *rhythmus.* Examine these words carefully. The origin of the English words (does, does not) account for the silent letter. _____

h

10. *Exhaurire* means to draw out, so if a long car ride draws one out, it ex___austs him.

exhaust

11. To tire one out is to ex_____ him.

exhaust

12. The legislator will soon _____ his listeners.

rhythm

13. The Latin word *rhythmus* means recurring motion or measure, so the English word meaning a regular beat in music is _____thm.

rhythm

14. The three basics of music are melody, harmony, and _____.

rhythm

15. Some modern artists have an altogether new sense of _____.

rhythm   exhaust

16. The monotonous _____ of the windshield wiper will eventually annoy and _____ the elderly driver.

knowledge

17. If *know* means to learn and understand, the understanding gained through experience and study is _____ledge.

first

18. The silent letter in the word that means understanding or learning is at the beginning of which syllable? _____

knowledge

19. He surprises me with his _____.

knowledge

20. Despite all his _____, he is quite illogical at times.

REVIEW

a. Wednesday
b. doubt
c. debts
d. rhythm
e. undoubtedly
f. exhaust
g. knowledge
h. subtle

21. Write the silent letter words for these sentences.

a. What day precedes Thursday? _____

b. How long will you _____ his motives?

      hesitate over

c. You owe far too many _____.

d. The three essentials of music are melody, harmony, and _____.

e. He is _____ the finest jazz trombonist

      without hesitation
today.

f. I am afraid that a long journey will _____

                        tire out
my grandfather.

g. Sometimes a little _____ is a handicap.

                learning

h. The distinction between the two is quite _____.

n

22. When you pronounce the verb *condemn*, which letter is not sounded? _____

yes

23. The word comes from the Latin *condemnare*. Is the silent letter related to the original word? _____

condemns

24. The Latin word means to damage, so if one "damages" another, he expresses severe disapproval of him—in other words, he con_____ him.

condemn

25. To censure or criticize severely is to _____.

condemned

26. Even before the trial, he was called a _____ed man.

end

27. Unlike the word *knowledge*, *condemn* has the silent letter at the _____ of the word.

p

28. Three words, *psychology*, *psychiatry*, and *psychopathy* are derived from the Greek word *psukhe*. Each word has the silent letter _____.

psychology

29. *Psukhe* means life, breath, soul, and *ology* is an ending meaning study. From these two is produced the word meaning the study of the mind or mental processes _____.

psychiatry

30. Since the ending *iatry* indicates medical treatment, the treatment of the mind is called _____.

psychopathy

31. The ending *pathy* indicates disease. Mental disorder can be called _____*opathy.*

psychology
psychiatry
psychopathy

32. The study of mental processes is _____;
the medical treatment of the mind is _____;
and a form of mental disease is _____.

u

33. The words *guard* and *guardian* have a common derivation: from Old French *garder* or *guarder*, from the Germanic. Here you find a shift in the spelling of the French verb, but the English words have retained the silent _____.

guard guardian

34. To watch over is the meaning of the word _____;
and the one who watches over is called a _____ian.

guard

35. To take precautions is also the meaning of the root word: the hospital tries to _____ against infection.

guardhouse
guardroom

36. The detention house for military personnel is called a _____house; the room in which prisoners are confined is a _____room.

writes

37. The last word to be studied is one of the most common in the English language and also one of the most often misspelled. It is derived from Old English *writan* meaning to tear or scratch. If one scratches out a messages, he _____ it.

is w

38. The Old English word for tear or scratch indicates that the origin of the current word (is, is not) responsible for the inclusion of the silent letter _____.

write
writing writer

39. The verb that means to form words and sentences is _____. The act of putting this down is _____ing, and the person who puts it down is the _____er.

w t

40. All three words have the silent ____ and only one ____ after the *i.*

writers
writing

41. Both my father and brothers are famous _____;
in fact, they are _____ novels at present.

a. condemn
b. psychology
c. guardian
d. writers
e. psychiatry
f. guard
g. writing
h. psychopathy

REVIEW

42. Complete or write the silent letter word for each sentence.

a. Some people like to con_____ before knowing the facts.
   criticize

b. My cousin is majoring in _____.
   study of the mind

c. My aunt now needs a legal _____.
   protector

d. We have several _____ in the family.
   authors

e. Medical treatment of the mind is called _____iatry.

f. To watch over is to _____.

g. The young boy is _____ a short story.
   composing

h. One form of mental disorder is _____opathy.

POSTTEST

From the meaning of each sentence, or the meaning clue, supply the correct silent letter word.

1. To protect is to _____.

2. A difficult art to master is the art of _____ing.

3. The study of the mental processes is _____.

4. To hesitate believing a person is to _____ him.

5. The day after Tuesday is _____.

6. The rain fell in a steady _____.
   measure or beat

7. He tried to impress us with his _____.
   learning

8. The girl bought so many articles on time that she was always in _____.

9. To criticize severely is to _____.

10. A legal protector is usually called a _____.

11. A person clever enough to make extremely fine distinctions is said to be _____.

12. Beyond hesitation is the definition of _____.

13. To tire out is the meaning of _____.

14. One who writes is a _____.

15. The medical treatment of the problems of the mind is _____.

Chapter 5

VOWEL STRESS

Perhaps one of the biggest problems in spelling is trying to identify vowel sounds when they are not distinct. At times correct pronunciation does help because we do mispronounce or slur vowels. Most of the time, however, vowel sounds that cause trouble cannot be classified as long or short sounds, or even approaching one or the other. For example, because the first *i* in *definite* receives little stress, making it unrecognizable as any kind of "i" sound, the word is often misspelled. Such unstressed sounds (or reduced vowels as they are sometimes called) appear in many words, so it is important for you to recognize this problem.

In this chapter, then, you will (1) become aware of the difficulties that unstressed (or lightly stressed) vowels present; (2) recognize these sounds and the syllables in which they appear; (3) spell a number of useful words with such vowel sounds, both in and out of context; and (4) from various contexts or definitions, reproduce the specific words in the chapter. In addition, it is hoped that you will become doubly conscious of unstressed and lightly stressed vowels and apply what you learn here to the spelling of other words.

PRETEST

Fill in the missing letter(s).

1. ben__fit
2. gramm__r
3. opt__mism
4. famil_____
5. hum__rous
6. compar__tive
7. r__diculous
8. elim__nate
9. sim__lar
10. dom__nant
11. warr__nt
12. cand__date
13. sent__nce
14. mand__tory
15. dorm__tory

16. math__matics

17. sacr__fice

18. contr__versy

19. __pinion

20. crit__cism

21. sep__rate

22. def__nite

23. calend__r

24. legit__mate

25. cat__gory

26. d__vide

27. prob__bly

28. fasc__nate

29. partic__l__r

30. priv__lege

31. lab__ratory

32. pecul_____

33. bull__tin

34. intell__gence

---

does

1. The first syllable of *ridiculous* (ri) has a slightly stressed vowel. If you mispronounce or slur this word you may choose the wrong vowel to represent the sound. First pronounce the word: ri dic u lous. In the second syllable *dic* the *i* has a short *i* sound as in *pick*. The first *i* (does, does not) have the same sound.

short

2. If you said "does not" you undoubtedly slurred that first *i*. In spelling this word, always remember that the vowel in the first and second syllables has the (long, short) sound of *i*. _____

ridiculous

3. Silly or laughable is one definition of _____ulous.

ridiculous

4. Deserving or inspiring ridicule is also a definition of

_____.

short

5. Like *ridiculous*, the word *divide* has a first vowel sound that must be correctly spoken and heard. And like the first syllable in *ridiculous*, the first syllable in this word has the (long, short) sound of *i*. _____

divide

6. To separate into parts is the meaning of _____vide.

divide

7. If no agreement in policy is reached, the assembly will _____ into factions.

pin (second)
o (first)

8. Like the slightly stressed vowel, the vowel that receives the least amount of stress in a word or hardly any stress at all, causes a problem. Take *opinion*, for example. Pronounce it and indicate which syllable receives the most stress: o pin ion. _____. Which syllable receives the least stress? _____

o

9. Since the vowel is not easily recognized as an o you must, in spelling the word, stress the letter in some way. Like this: opinion—or perhaps connect it with the verb *opine*, meaning to think. *Opine* has a distinct sound of the vowel ___.

opinion

10. A conclusion one holds or an evaluation based on special knowledge are two definitions of _____.

tic (second)
little

11. Now take the word *particular*. It is syllabified like this: par tic u lar. Say the word quickly, noting how much stress each syllable receives. Which syllable receives the most? _____
Do the other syllables have (some or little) stress? _____

par (first) lar (last)

12. Since unstressed vowels are not easy to distinguish, pronunciation alone may not solve the problem. Emphasizing the vowel sounds and looking at the word carefully will help. Which syllables are similar: par tic u lar?
_____.

particular

13. Now write the word from memory: _____.

particular

14. A specific event can be called a _____ one.

no
rant (second or last)

15. Pronounce *warrant*. Does the a sound the same in both syllables war rant? _____ Which syllable has the unstressed vowel? _____

wAr rAnt

16. Though it is difficult to distinguish this vowel sound, you can remember it this way: wAr r__nt

warrant

17. A guarantee or written authorization is a _____.

last
a
mar dar lar

18. Three common and useful words having the same problems are *grammar, calendar,* and *similar*. First, look at the syllables: gram mar   cal en dar   sim i lar. The unstressed vowel appears in which syllable of each word? _____
What is the vowel? _____
Not only do these words have this similarity, they also have a graphic similarity: gram_____ calen_____ simi_____

grammar

19. From the Latin word *gramma*, meaning letter, comes the English word _____.

calendar

20. From the medieval Latin word *Kalendarium*, a money lender's account book, comes the English _____.

similar

21. To be related in appearance is to be sim_____.

a. calendar
b. grammar
c. similar

22. Supply each of these three words according to the context.

a. I have noted all my appointments on the _____.

b. Depending on the method of presentation, the study of _____ can be interesting.

c. The two plays have _____ plots.

last
iar (or *liar*)

23. *Familiar* and *peculiar* also have an unstressed vowel and a graphic similarity. Pronounce them. What same syllable in each word has the least stress, (first, second, last)? _____ What is the graphic similarity? _____

liar
iar

24. To be unusual or strange is to be pecu_____.
Common, or well-known is the definition of *famil*_____.

familiar
peculiar

25. We are now on a _____ road. He acts in a most _____ manner.

lar liar

26. Do not confuse these endings: simi_____ and fami_____.

last
e

27. Look at and then pronounce the word *sentence*. Which syllable has the unstressed vowel (first, last)? _____
Both the first and last syllables have which vowel? _____

sentences

28. A paragraph can be monotonous reading if all the s_____ are the same length.

REVIEW

a. *a a*   g. *lar*
b. *a*   h. *dar*
c. *iar*   i. *iar*
d. *i*   j. *o*
e. *a*   k. *e e*
f. *i*

29. Fill in the missing letters.

a. p___rticul___r   g. simi_____

b. gramm___r   h. calen_____

c. famil_____   i. pecul_____

d. r___diculous   j. ___pinion

e. warr___nt   k. s___nt___nce

f. d___vide

mar dar lar
iar iar
ridiculous
divide
a a
a a
e e

30. Three words with similar endings are *gram*_____, *calen*_____, and *simi*_____.
Two words with similar endings are *famil*_____ and *pecul*_____.
Two words with the same vowel sound in the first syllable are _____*diculous* and _____*vide*.
Three words having the same vowel in their first and last syllables are w___rr___nt, p___rticul___r, and s___nt___nce.

a a a da	**31.** An unstressed vowel in the middle of a word can often cause difficulties. Most of the problems are with the *i*, but some common and useful words have *e*, *o*, or *a* problems. Four with bothersome *a*'s are *separate*, *probably*, *comparative*, and *mandatory*. The words are syllabified like this: sep a rate, prob a bly, com par a tive, man da to ry. Pronounce them, noting the amount of stress placed on each syllable. Write the syllable of each word that has the unstressed vowel: _____ _____ _____ _____.
separate	**32.** If something is detached or disjointed it is sep_____.
separate	**33.** If the committees do not meet together, they hold _____ meetings.
probably	**34.** Most likely is the definition of the word *prob*_____.
probably	**35.** The storms will _____ damage many houses.
mandatory	**36.** From the Latin *mandatum*, meaning a command, comes the word _____*tory*.
mandatory	**37.** Attendance at all lectures is _____.
third	**38.** Pronounce the word *comparative*. Although the two vowels in the middle of the word are the same, the unstressed *a* is in the (second, third) syllable. _____
comparative	**39.** If something can be estimated by comparison, it is said to be compar_____.
comparative	**40.** *Bigger* is the com_____ form of *big*.
a da a a	**41.** What are the missing letters in these words: sep__rate man_____tory prob__bly compar__tive
second second second second	**42.** Four common words often misspelled because of their *e* problem are *benefit, bulletin, category, mathematics*. Perform this operation mentally: say the words according to syllables, noting the amount of stress for each. In which syllable of *benefit* is the unstressed vowel? _____ in bulletin? _____ in category? _____ and in mathematics? _____

a. benefit
b. category
c. bulletin
d. mathematics

43. a. To be helpful or to improve is the definition of ben_____.

b. A class or a specifically designated division is called a cat_____.

c. A periodical published by an organization is sometimes called a bul_____.

d. The study of numbers and associated relationships is math_____.

a. bulletin
b. mathematics
c. category
d. benefit

44. Read these sentences for their meaning, then supply the correct "e" word for each.

a. How often does the company _____ come out?

b. What was your grade in the _____ course?

c. Do you intend to list all items in each _____?

d. A performance presented to raise money for charity is a _____.

second
o

45. Now let us turn to another group of words: *humorous, controversy, laboratory.* First pronounce them, dividing them into syllables. Which same syllable in each has the unstressed vowel (first, second, third)? _____
These words have which vowel problem? _____

a. humorous
b. controversy
c. laboratory

46. a. Laughable or comical is the definition of the adjective hu_____.

b. A dispute, especially a lengthy one, is a con_____versy.

c. A room equipped for scientific experimentation is a lab_____atory.

a. humorous
b. laboratory
c. controversy

47. Supply the correct "o" word for these sentences.

a. On our travels we saw many _____ sights.

b. My cousin works in a _____.

c. The new tax issue has started a _____ between the major political parties.

controversy
laboratory
humorous

48. A long dispute is a _____;
an experimentation room is a _____;
a comical picture is a _____ one.

REVIEW

49. Fill in the missing letters.

a. *a*
b. e
c. o
d. *a*
e. *a*
f. e
g. o
h. e
i. *a*
j. o
k. e

a. sep__rate   g. hum__rous

b. ben__fit   h. math__matics

c. contr__versy   i. mand__tory

d. compar__tive   j. lab__ratory

e. prob__bly   k. cat__gory

f. bull__tin

second
i i

50. Let us turn to these words: *definite* and *dominant*. Here are two common words frequently used in writing and just as frequently misspelled. Look at, pronounce, and mentally syllabify both words. In which syllable is the unstressed vowel (first, second, third)? _____ Write the second syllable for each word: _____ _____

definite
dominant

51. To be specific is to be def_____; to be outstanding is to be dom_____.

dominant
definite

52. From the Latin *dominans* comes the English word _____; from the Latin *definire* comes the English _____.

definite

53. She had a _____ reason for arriving late.
                    specific

dominant

54. Of all the characteristics attributed to the one cause, the last one is _____.
                    outstanding

first
second *i*

55. The following four words are grouped together because they have a similar "rhythmic ring" and may be more easily remembered this way. Take *candidate* and *fascinate*. Each has three syllables. The major stress comes in which syllable of both words (first, second, third)? _____ The unstressed vowel is in which syllable of both words? _____ The vowel is ____.

candidate
fascinate

56. A person who seeks an office is a can____date. To spellbind or to attract irresistibly is the definition of *fas____ate*.

candidate
fascinate

57. Although his lack of education may prevent his being a _____, his ability to tell a story will
                    office-seeker
_____a wide audience.
        attract

third *i*

58. Two others with a rhythmic ring are *eliminate* and *legitimate*. Let us syllabify them first: e lim i nate, le git i mate. Which syllable in both has the un-stressed vowel? _____ The troublesome vowel is _____.

legitimate eliminate

59. If something is lawful, it is le_____mate. If you wish to get rid of something, you want to elim___nate it.

legitimate

60. A solution that is based on logical reasoning or is a legal solution is a _____ solution.

eliminate

61. Stiff competition can _____ athletes from the preliminaries.

eliminated
legitimate

62. Sometimes an athlete can be _____ from a race by means that are not _____.

second (*ti*)
second (*i*)

63. Two words having similar endings can be presented together: *optimism* and *criticism.* Pronounce them care-fully, listening to the stresses in each word. Of the three syllables in optimism, which has the unstressed vowel? _____ in criticism? _____

crit i cism
op ti mism

64. Now complete the last two syllables of each word: crit _____ _____   op _____ _____.

criticism
optimism

65. The act of making judgments is known as crit_____; tending to expect the best outcome is the definition of op_____.

criticism

66. To learn to write one must be open to _____.

optimism

67. Today there may be more people who express pessi-mism than _____.

i second

68. The troublesome vowel in *dormitory* is again the ____. It is in the _____ syllable.

dormitory

69. From the Latin *dormitorium* comes the English word _____.

dormitory

70. A building to house a number of students can be called a _____.

third (l*i*)

71. *Intelligence* is a common word and it is just as com-monly misspelled, mainly because of its unstressed vowel. Pronounce the word and mentally divide it into syllables. In which syllable is the vowel to watch out for? _____

intelligence

72. The ability to acquire and apply knowledge, and information or news received, are two definitions of the word intel_____.

intelligence

73. The psychologist claims that Marty has superior

_____.

3
second
ri   i

74. And here are the last two words: *sacrifice* and *privilege*. Pronounce them, noting the syllables as you do. How many syllables does each have? _____ Both have the unstressed vowel in which syllable? _____ That syllable is sac_____fice and priv____lege.

sacrifice
privilege

75. To offer up something or to sell or give away at a loss is to sac_____; a special advantage or benefit can be called a priv_____.

privileges
sacrifice

76. Because the young ruler was not content with the _____s he already had, he was forced to _____ all his expensive possessions.

REVIEW

a. dominant
b. privilege
c. definite
d. candidate
e. legitimate
f. criticism
g. intelligence
h. fascinate
i. eliminate
j. optimism
k. dormitory
l. sacrifice

77. From the meaning of the sentence and other clues complete the spelling of these "vowel" words.

a. To be outstanding is to be dom_____.

b. A special advantage is a _____.

c. A specific proposal is a def_____ one.

d. Do you think the can_____ will continue to attract many voters?

e. A lawful course is a _____ one.

f. The book reviewer is known for his fair crit_____.

g. The ability to acquire and apply knowledge is called in_____.

h. His Irish brogue continues to fas_____ me.

i. How many words can you elim_____ without affecting the meaning?

j. No matter how serious the problem is, my grandfather believes that op_____ is the best attitude to have.

k. Are you living in the new _____?

l. Every winter the natives sac_____ their most productive animal.

POSTTEST

From the clues given below write the complete words.

1. ben_____ improve
2. dor_____ building to house students
3. ___pinion conclusion
4. sac_____ offering
5. pe_____ unusual or strange
6. sen_____ grammatical unit
7. hu_____ comical
8. def_____ specific
9. crit_____ judgments made
10. war_____ guarantee
11. lab_____ room for experimentation
12. can_____ office-seeker
13. ____diculous silly or laughable
14. cal_____ table showing days of the year
15. prob_____ likely
16. bul_____ periodical
17. le_____ lawful
18. man_____ required
19. fam_____ well known
20. com_____tive estimated by comparison
21. cat_____ designated division
22. dom_____ outstanding
23. ____vide separate
24. gram_____ study of language
25. math_____ study of numbers
26. con_____versy dispute
27. fas_____ attract
28. op_____ hopeful attitude
29. sep_____ detached or disjointed
30. priv_____ special advantage
31. sim_____ related
32. partic_____ specific
33. elim_____ get rid of
34. intel_____ information received, mental ability

Chapter 6

SOUND-ALIKE SUFFIXES

Is *able* correct, or is it *ible*? Should it be *ary* or *ery*, *ance* or *ence*? When suffix alternatives sound alike, how can you tell which one is right? As you know, questions like these arise daily, and without some forthcoming answers, it is difficult to spell words with these suffixes accurately. This chapter will help you answer these and similar questions. For some of these elements there are rules; for others, there are only tendencies for certain vowels or consonants to take this or that ending. But whether they are rules or tendencies, they will guide you to better spelling.

In this chapter you will learn to (1) apply rules or follow tendencies in the spelling of a number of useful words with suffixes; (2) practice and use these words in and out of context; (3) identify those words that do not follow rules or tendencies; and (4) from stated definitions, recognize and write the required words. In addition, this chapter will furnish a background needed for spelling other words with troublesome suffixes, and stimulate your curiosity about language in general.

PRETEST

Choose the correct ending for each of the following.

A. able-ible

1. permiss_____
2. accept_____
3. estim_____
4. change_____
5. admir_____

6. market_____
7. inevit_____
8. elig_____
9. consider_____
10. pass_____

11. poss_____   14. repress_____

12. perish_____   15. reduc_____

13. defens_____   16. educ_____

B. *ary-ery*

1. bound_____   5. cemet_____

2. station_____ (writing paper)   6. Febru_____

3. secret_____   7. contempor_____

4. libr_____   8. station_____ (fixed)

C. *ise-ize-yze*

1. adv_____   6. emphas_____

2. anal_____   7. paral_____

3. critic_____   8. exerc_____

4. summar_____   9. advert_____

5. surpr_____   10. real_____

D. *ance-ence*

1. intellig_____ (*ent, ant*)   13. mainten_____ (*ance, ence*)

2. resist_____ (*ance, ence*)   14. excell_____ (*ent, ant*)

3. equival_____ (*ent, ant*)   15. guid_____ (*ance, ence*)

4. accid_____ (*ant, ent*)   16. influ_____ (*ence, ance*)

5. defend_____ (*ant, ent*)   17. extravag_____ (*ance, ence*)

6. promin_____ (*ance, ence*)   18. insist_____ (*ent, ant*)

7. exist_____ (*ant, ent*)   19. attend_____ (*ance, ence*)

8. confid_____ (*ence, ance*)   20. domin_____ (*ant, ent*)

9. sci_____ (*ence, ance*)   21. preval_____ (*ence, ance*)

10. consequ_____ (*ent, ant*)   22. descend_____ (*ant, ent*)

11. experi_____ (*ence, ance*)   23. brilli_____ (*ance, ence*)

12. magnific_____ (*ence, ance*)   24. signific_____ (*ent, ant*)

ABLE - IBLE

able
all are complete words
horr is just a base,
not a complete word

1. Generally, if the root is a full word it will take the suffix *able*. For example, *eat, drink,* and *read* are complete words, so they take *able:* eatable, drinkable, readable. Conversely, if the root is not a full word, it will usually take *ible*. In *permissible* and *possible* the bases are *permiss* and *poss*. Since they are not complete, the *ible* ending is correct. Which ending would the following take: *laugh   accept   lament   commend?* _____
State your reason briefly. _____
_____

Why does *horrible* have *ible* and not *able?* _____
_____

a. justifiable
b. playable
c. rectifiable
d. employable

2. Complete words ending in y preceded by a vowel also take *able*. For instance, *enjoy* ends in *oy*, so *enjoy + able = enjoyable*. Now take *rely*. It is also a complete word, but it ends in y preceded by a consonant (*l*). Usually words like *rely* change the y to i before a suffix beginning with a vowel, *rely + ed = relied*. Although *ible* also begins with a vowel, adding it to *reli* would produce a peculiar looking and sounding word ("unreliiable"). So you must add *able: reliable*. Now add the suffix and write the complete words.

a. justify   _____   c. rectify   _____

b. play   _____   d. employ   _____

a. marketable
b. perishable
c. multipliable
d. comfortable
e. employable
f. variable
g. taxable
h. enjoyable
i. agreeable
j. pitiable

3. Apply what you have learned so far by choosing the correct suffix—*able* or *ible*—and writing the complete words.

a. market   _____   f. vary   _____

b. perish   _____   g. tax   _____

c. multiply   _____   h. enjoy   _____

d. comfort   _____   i. agree   _____

e. employ   _____   j. pity   _____

4. Another aid in choosing correctly between *able* and *ible* is to remember the related noun. Take a look at the two groups of words.

A.
commendation
consideration
admiration

B.
permission
admission
repression
perfection

ation
yes
ion
no
repress   perfect
both

What is the five-letter ending of each in group A? _____
Is the part of each word before this five-letter ending complete? (Remember that "silent e" words usually drop the e before a suffix beginning with a vowel.) _____
What is the three-letter ending of each word in group B?

_____

Is the part before this ending complete in each word? ____
Name the complete word(s) in Group B. _____

_____

The double s in the words in group B appears in (complete, incomplete, or both) words.

complete
ss

5. Even though there are only a few words in the above lists, we can point out some tendencies. The two nounal endings are important: *ation, ion.* The words in group A (*ation*) have (complete, incomplete) words within them?

_____

The words in group B (*ion*) are either complete or incomplete. The incomplete words have what double letter in the base? _____

able
ible
ible

6. Here are the same nouns as well as the *able-ible* adjectives relating to them.

A.

commendation	commendable
consideration	considerable
admiration	admirable

B.

permission	permissible
admission	admissible
repression	repressible
perfection	perfectible

Again, we can make some generalizations (not rules, you notice).
If a noun is formed by adding *ation,* the adjective will probably be formed by adding (*able, ible*). _____
If *ion* is the ending for the noun, the ending for the adjective will undoubtedly be (*able, ible*). _____
Whether in a complete or incomplete word, the double s will usually take (*able, ible*). _____

a

7. An exception to the "completeness" idea for *able* is the word *evitable,* and its negative *inevitable,* derived from the Latin verb *evitare,* meaning to avoid. Very often the spelling of the original word governs the spelling of the English derivative. Look carefully at the ending of the Latin verb. Which letter tells you to add *able* or *ible* to the incomplete forms *evit* and *inevit*? _____

evitable
inevitable

8. Now write these two exceptions:
_____ and _____.

complete
do
do not
repression

9. Look at these words: *kiss, pass,* and *repress.*
All are (complete, incomplete) words. _____
All (do, do not) have an *ss.* _____
All (do, do not) have a related noun ending in *ion.* _____
Name the related noun(s). _____

ion

10. Since *repress* has a double *s and* a related *ion* noun,
it takes *ible* to form the adjective. Since *kiss* and *pass*
do not have related nouns ending in *ion,* they take *able.*
So before adding *able* or *ible* to a word having *ss,* you
must first determine if that word has a related noun
ending in _____.

a. kissable
b. passable
c. repressible

11. Form the adjectives from these words by adding *able*
or *ible:*

a. kiss _____   b. pass _____   c. repress _____

no
no
yes

12. In addition to the double *s,* an *ns* at the end of a
base can alert you to add *ible.* But again you should
determine if there is a related noun and what its ending is.
Here are three bases:
defens   respons   dispens
Is there a related noun for *defens?* _____
How about *respons?* _____
And *dispens?* _____

able

13. Since *defens* and *respons* do not have related nouns,
they will follow the general tendency for *ns* to take *ible.*
The related noun for *dispens* is *dispensation.* Which ending will the adjective take (*able, ible*)? _____

a. responsible
b. dispensable
c. defensible

14. Form the adjectives by choosing *able* or *ible.*

a. respons_____   b. dispens_____   c. defens_____

15. On page 56 is a list of words to which you can add *ation*
or *ion* to form the related noun and then *able* or *ible*
to form the adjective. Apply what you have learned so far
and complete the words for both columns. If no word is
appropriate write "none." Watch the "silent e" words as
the e is usually dropped before the vowel suffix.

a. destruction
   destructible
b. none
   passable
c. imagination
   imaginable
d. corruption
   corruptible
e. accession
   accessible
f. admission
   admissible
g. consolation
   consolable
h. none
   inevitable
i. perfection
   perfectible
j. dispensation
   dispensable

Root or base	Noun	Adjective
a. destruct	_____	_____
b. pass	_____	_____
c. imagine	_____	_____
d. corrupt	_____	_____
e. access	_____	_____
f. admiss	_____	_____
g. console	_____	_____
h. inevit	_____	_____
i. perfect	_____	_____
j. dispens	_____	_____

a. S
b. S
c. S
d. H
e. H
f. H
g. S
h. S

16. The sound of c and g at the end of a complete word or a base can also suggest the correct ending.
The soft sound of c is like an s (as in *city*).
The hard sound of c is like a k (as in *category*).
The hard sound of g is like the g in *go* or *get*.
Pronounce the words below and identify by S or H if the underlined portions are soft or hard sounds.

a. peace	_____		e. drag	_____
b. change	_____		f. destruction	_____
c. reduce	_____		g. eligible	_____
d. educate	_____		h. lace	_____

soft
ce
able
able
g (no e)
hard
able

17. Look at and pronounce these two groups of words.

A.   B.

legible   revocable
serviceable   educable
noticeable
enforceable
changeable

Group A.
What sound of c or g do you have here? _____
Each with the soft c has what two-letter ending before the suffix? _____
Each word with ce takes (*able, ible*). _____
The word with ge at the end of the root takes (*able, ible*).

_____

The word with the soft g and suffix *ible* has (g, ge) as its ending? _____

Group B.
What sound of c do you have here? _____
What ending does each word have? _____

able
ible
able
able

18. Using just a few words from the same list as illustrations, let us develop some generalizations.

legible   serviceable
changeable   educable

Words having a soft *g* in *ge* at the end of the root word take (*able, ible*). _____
Those having a soft *g* at the end of the base take (*able, ible*). _____
Those having a soft *c* in *ce* at the end of the root word take (*able, ible*). _____
Those having a hard *c* take (*able, ible*). _____

a. serviceable
b. educable
c. eligible
d. enforceable
e. changeable
f. legible
g. revocable
h. reducible
i. deducible

19. Pronounce these *able-ible* words, look at the ending of the bases, then write the complete word.

a. service_____   f. leg_____

b. educ_____   g. revoc_____

c. elig_____   h. reduc_____

d. enforce_____   i. deduc_____

e. change_____

REVIEW

able

20. Generally, full or complete words, like *commend* or *market*, take (*able, ible*). _____

a. *able*
b. *able*

21. Which ending (*able, ible*) would you add to

a. complete words ending in *y*, like *enjoy?* _____

b. complete words ending in *y*, like *comply?* _____

change y to i

22. In adding *able* to *comply*, you must first _____ .

able

23. Generally, words ending in *ce* or *ge* (like *service* or *change*) take (*able, ible*)? _____

a. soft
b. *ible*
c. there is no ce or
   ge—just c and g

24. In your mind add the *able-ible* ending to these bases and pronounce them as complete words: leg_____
reduc_____

a. Each has the (soft, hard) sound of c or g? _____

b. Each takes (*able, ible*)? _____

c. Why did you choose this ending? _____

_____

a. remissible
b. perfectible
c. dispensable
d. corruptible
e. revocable
f. consolable
g. admissible
h. irritable

25. Look at the endings of these nouns and then write the related adjectives.

a. remission _____   e. revocation _____

b. perfection _____   f. consolation _____

c. dispensation _____   g. admission _____

d. corruption _____   h. irritation _____

evitable
inevitable

26. Finish the spelling by adding *able* or *ible*.

evit_____   inevit_____

ible

27. The consonants *ns*, as in *defens* and *respons* take (*able, ible*)? _____

able

28. Because *dispens* has the related noun dispensation, the *ns* takes (*able, ible*)? _____

noun ending in *ation*
so adjective is *able*;
the *c* is hard

29. Look at and pronounce these two nouns: *education, revocation*.
Give two reasons why *educable* and *revocable* take *able*.

_____

_____

a. accession
   accessible
b. irritation
   irritable
c. impression
   impressible
d. consideration
   considerable
e. digestion
   digestible
f. none
   creditable
g. detestation
   detestable
h. variation
   variable
i. none
   understandable

30. For the following complete and incomplete words write (1) the related noun (if none, write "none") and (2) the correct *able-ible* adjective.

Root or base	Noun	Adjective
a. access	_____	_____
b. irritate	_____	_____
c. impress	_____	_____
d. consider	_____	_____
e. digest	_____	_____
f. credit	_____	_____
g. detest	_____	_____
h. vary	_____	_____
i. understand	_____	_____

a. serviceable
b. eligible
c. permissible
d. reducible
e. inevitable
f. changeable
g. educable
h. horrible
i. responsible
j. despicable

31. Complete these with *able* or *ible*.

a. service_____   f. change_____

b. elig_____   g. educ_____

c. permiss_____   h. horr_____

d. reduc_____   i. respons_____

e. inevit_____   j. despic_____

---

ery

ARY - ERY

32. Definition and association of ideas can often help you remember whether the ending is *ary* or *ery*. For example, writing paper is called *stationery*. If you hesitate in spelling this word, remember that it has the same ending as paper.

Another commonly misspelled word can be remembered by its definition. A corpse is usually buried in a grave and the site for many graves is called a graveyard, or cemet_____.

cemetery
stationery

33. Complete these definitions:
A place for burying the dead is a cem_____; writing paper is called sta_____.

a. stationery
b. cemetery

34. Complete these sentences:

a. For thank-you notes, Susie bought pink _____.

b. Michael helped put in tombstones at the _____.

boundary
library
secretary
February
contemporary

35. Since *stationery* and *cemetery* are the two commonly misspelled *ery* words, complete the spelling of the following:

bound_____   Febru_____

libr_____   contempor_____

secret_____

contemporary
library
February
boundary
secretary
stationary

36. The word meaning modern or present day is *contem*
_____.
A place where books are deposited is a li_____.
The second month of the year is Feb_____.
A limit is a bound_____.
A girl who types and takes shorthand can be called a secre_____.
A seat that is not movable is station_____.

stationary

37. If writing paper is *stationery*, the word meaning fixed, not movable, is _____.

38. Now write the words that match the definitions.

a. boundary
b. stationary
c. library
d. contemporary
e. secretary
f. February

a. limit   _____

b. fixed   _____

c. book depository _____

d. present day   _____

e. one who types _____

f. second month   _____

REVIEW

paper

39. To spell *stationery* correctly, what word do you associate with it? _____

e

40. What one vowel goes in each blank? c___m___t___ry

ary

41. You always end the name of the second month with *ary* or *ery*? _____

secretary

42. A girl who types and takes dictation is a _____.

ISE - IZE - YZE

surprise
arise
exercise

43. It is not the purpose here to supply the derivations of words ending in *ise, ize,* or *yze.* Suffice it to say that many come from Old French and Latin, hence *ise*; and many come from the Greek, hence *ize* and *yze.* Because of their common origin, the "ise" words are grouped together and because association helps you to remember, the words will be related in what can be called "association sentences."
Here is the first:
It should be no *surprise* that I *exercise* when I *arise.*
There are two words with two syllables:

_____   _____

The third has three: _____

r
2

44. *Surprise* and *exercise* are often misspelled in other parts of the words as well. For example, what consonant appears twice in the first word? _____
In the second syllable of the second word are there (2 or 3) letters? _____

surprise
exercise

45. To fill with wonder or disbelief is the meaning of *sur_____. To practice* means to ex_____.

arise

46. The word to get up is a_____.

a. surprise
b. exercise
c. arise

47. Read the sentences below and supply the three words just studied.

a. He will _____ us all some day.

b. Athletes must _____ every day to keep fit.

c. I _____ at six-thirty.

surprise
exercise
arise

48. Now back to our original sentence:
It should be no _____ that I_____
when I _____.

advise
enterprise
supervise
advertise
merchandise

49. Let us put some *ise* words into a business setting:
Investing in an *enterprise* may mean having to *advise* and *supervise* a number of employees, and to *advertise* the *merchandise*.
The one word with two syllables is _____.
The rest have three syllables each:

_____   _____

_____   _____

enterprise
supervise
advertise
merchandise

50. A business venture is called an enter_____.
To direct or inspect is to super_____. To make a public announcement is to ad_____. Goods or wares are known as mer_____.

enterprise
advise
supervise
advertise
merchandise

51. Let us return to our original sentence: Investing in an _____ may mean having to _____
and _____ a number of employees, and to _____ the _____.

yze

52. Now look at this group of words.

realize   criticize
emphasize   characterize
recognize   summarize
analyze   paralyze

Of the eight words above, only two have which ending (*ize, yze*)? _____

analyze
paralyze

53. To separate a whole into its parts and examine them is the meaning of *anal_____; to render ineffective, or to unnerve is the meaning of *paral_____.

analyze
paralyze

54. These two words are similar in another respect:
an____yze   par____yze

a. paralyze
b. analyze

55. Supply the correct *yze* word:

a. Some forms of polio will _____ an individual.

b. To reach an effective solution you should first _____ the problem.

analyze   paralyze

56. The two words ending in *yze* are _____ and _____.

re al ize
em pha size

57. For the "ize" words let us continue "association sentences." Two go nicely together:
Did you *realize* you didn't *emphasize* the right points in your argument? Here is the first syllable for each—you write the rest.
re _____ _____   em _____ _____

realize
emphasize

58. To understand clearly, or to accomplish is to re_____. To stress or to achieve is to em_____.

a. realize
b. emphasize
c. realize

59. Write the correct *ize* word:

a. I do _____ what you are saying.

b. You should _____ your main points.

c. Some day he may _____ his dream.

realize
emphasize

60. To return to our original sentence: Did you _____ that you didn't _____ the right points in your argument?

3
rec og nize
crit i cize

61. Here is our next sentence:
Even though you *recognize* his faults, you don't need to *criticize* him publicly.
Each word has _____ syllables. Complete the syllables for each:
rec _____ _____   crit _____ _____

recognize
criticize

62. To take notice is to rec_____.
To judge or evaluate is to crit_____.

criticize

63. Of these two words which one often carries the idea of simply finding fault? _____

recognize

64. If you are aware that you have seen a particular person before, you _____ him.

recognize
criticize

65. Even though you _____ his faults, you don't have to _____ him publicly.

summarize
characterize

66. The last two important words are *summar*_____ and *character*_____.

characterize
summarize

67. To describe the qualities of or give character to is the definition of the word _____.
To sum or to restate briefly is to _____.

a. characterize
b. summarize
c. characterize

68. Write the correct one of these two for each sentence.

a. His temper and his bad manners _____ him as a boor.

b. Now _____ your main ideas.

c. How would you _____ Mr. Jones?

REVIEW

a. *ize*   i. *ize*
b. *yze*   j. *ise*
c. *ise*   k. *ize*
d. *ize*   l. *ise*
e. *ise*   m. *yze*
f. *ise*   n. *ise*
g. *ize*   o. *ise*
h. *ise*   p. *ize*

69. Choose the correct ending *ize-yze-ise* for these words:

a. real_____   i. character_____

b. anal_____   j. merchand_____

c. advert_____   k. recogn_____

d. emphas_____   l. exerc_____

e. surpr_____   m. paral_____

f. adv_____   n. superv_____

g. critic_____   o. ar_____

h. enterpr_____   p. summar_____

ANCE - ENCE

existence
insistence
consistence
persistence
competence

70. There are no rules to guide you in adding the suffixes *ance* (*ant*) or *ence* (*ent*). Certain consonants, however, tend to take the *a* or the *e*. The consonants *t* and *v* tend toward the *a*: accept—acceptance; import—importance; relev—relevance. But some *t*'s do not:
exist   insist   consist   persist   compet
If accept, import, and relev take *ance*, add the correct ending to the five exceptions, and write the complete words:

_____   _____

_____   _____

_____

existence
competence
insistence
consistence
persistence

71. Association can help you to remember these exceptions.
First you must exist, so you have exist_____. Last, you have sufficiency or compet_____. In between are the various stages of striving:
_ _ _sist_____   _ _ _sist_____   _ _ _sist_____

existence
insistence
consistence
persistence
competence

72. Name these five exceptions.

_____   _____
_____   _____
_____

a. relevant
b. importance
c. insistent
d. resistance
e. competent
f. assistance
g. existent
h. acceptance
i. persistence
j. admittance
k. repentant
l. inheritance

73. Now apply what you have learned so far and add the correct suffix.

a. relev   (*ant, ent*)   _____

b. import   (*ance, ence*)   _____

c. insist   (*ant, ent*)   _____

d. resist   (*ance, ence*)   _____

e. compet   (*ent, ant*)   _____

f. assist   (*ance, ence*)   _____

g. exist   (*ent, ant*)   _____

h. accept   (*ance, ence*)   _____

i. persist   (*ence, ance*)   _____

j. admitt   (*ance, ence*)   _____

k. repent   (*ant, ent*)   _____

l. inherit   (*ance, ence*)   _____

a. S   d. S
b. H   e. H
c. S   f. S

74. The sound of the *c* and *g* will often govern which ending is correct. The hard sound of *c* (as in *cat*) and the hard sound of *g* (as in *go*) require *ance* or *ant*. The soft sound of *c* (as in *city*) and the soft sound of *g* (as in *gem*) take *ence* or *ent*.
Pronounce these words; then identify which sound each underlined consonant has. Use S (soft) or H (hard).

a. adolescent   _____   d. magnificent   _____

b. extravagance   _____   e. significance   _____

c. intelligence   _____   f. emergence   _____

ance
ent
ence

75. Look again at the list above.
The words with the hard *c* or *g* have which ending? _____
The words with the soft *c* have which ending? _____
The words with the soft *g* have which ending? _____

a. emergency
b. adolescent
c. extravagance
d. intelligent
e. significance
f. magnificent

76. Complete the spelling of these.

a. emerg_____ (ancy, ency) _____

b. adolesc_____ (ent, ant) _____

c. extravag_____ (ance, ence) _____

d. intellig_____ (ent, ant) _____

e. signific_____ (ance, ence) _____

f. magnific_____ (ant, ent) _____

REVIEW

a. intelligence
b. existence
c. important
d. insistence
e. acceptance
f. assistant
g. persistence
h. extravagant
i. consistency

77. Test your skill by adding the correct suffix and writing the complete word.

a. intellig_____ (ance, ence) _____

b. exist_____ (ence, ance) _____

c. import_____ (ent, ant) _____

d. insist_____ (ence, ance) _____

e. accept_____ (ence, ance) _____

f. assist_____ (ent, ant) _____

g. persist_____ (ence, ance) _____

h. extravag_____ (ant, ent) _____

i. consist_____ (ancy, ency) _____

ence
ance

78. Now look at these words carefully:

equivalent   eminence
excellence   imminence
prevalent   prominence
                    permanent

Both groups have *ence* or *ent*. In the first the consonant *l* precedes the ending and in the second it is *n*. But look at these: *balance, dominance, maintenance*. Here you also have *l* and *n* preceding the suffix, but it is *ance*, not *ence*. The two groups of words illustrates the tendency of *l* and *n* to take _____. The three exceptions take _____.

balance   dominance
maintenance

79. What are the three exceptions?

_____   _____   _____

a. *ence*   e. *ance*
b. *ance*   f. *ence*
c. *ence*   g. *ence*
d. *ence*   h. *ance*

80. Supply the correct suffix: *ance* or *ence*.

a. equival_____   e. bal_____

b. domin_____   f. perman_____

c. emin_____   g. immin_____

d. preval_____   h. mainten_____

a. excellence
b. equivalent
c. prevalent
d. balance
e. maintenance
f. imminent
g. permanent

81. Complete the word for each sentence.

a. When one strives for excell_____ he must
work hard.   *ence, ance*

b. Equal in substance or value is the meaning of
equival_____ .
           ant, ent

c. To be widespread is to be preval_____.
                   ant, ent

d. There should be bal_____ of power.
                ence, ance

e. The state of maintaining is called mainten_____.
                          ance, ence

f. A renowned person is immin_____.
                   ant, ent

g. Lasting is the definition of perman_____.
                       ant, ent

abundance
attendance
descendant
guidance
defendant

82. The consonant *d* tends to take the same ending as the consonants *l* and *n*. There are times, however, when it does not, and it is these "do nots" that are troublesome.
From the list below choose the "do nots" and write them.

superintendent   independence
accident   descendant
abundance   dependent
attendance   guidance
confidence   defendant
antecedent

_____

_____

_____

defendant
guidance
attendance
abundance
descendant

83. Let us try grouping to better remember them: The defend_____ needs guid_____. A large attend_____ suggests an abund_____. What proceeds from an ancestor is a descend_____.

a. descendant
b. defendant
c. superintendent
d. guidance
e. attendant
f. accidence
g. confidence
h. dependent
i. abundance
j. incident

84. Keeping these exceptions in mind, fill in the correct suffix.

a. descend_____ (ant, ent)

b. defend_____ (ant, ent)

c. superintend_____ (ant, ent)

d. guid_____ (ance, ence)

e. attend_____ (ant, ent)

f. accid_____ (ence, ance)

g. confid_____ (ence, ance)

h. depend_____ (ant, ent)

i. abund_____ (ance, ence)

j. incid_____ (ant, ent)

i
flu
qu

85. Look carefully at these groups.

A.	B.	C.
experience	influence	delinquent
convenience	affluence	consequent
ingredient		
science		

There is a single letter or two or more letters that are responsible for the *ence* or *ent* ending.
In group A what vowel is responsible?_____
In group B what two consonants plus a vowel are responsible? _____
In group C what consonant and a vowel are responsible?

_____

i flu
qu

86. In other words, the endings *ence* or *ent* usually follow the single vowel _____, the three letters _____, and the two letters _____.

ance   ant

87. One "i" word does not take the usual ending. Complete its spelling: brilli_____ or brilli_____.

brilliant
brilliance

88. To be full of light is to be _____; the extreme brightness or splendor is called _____.

a. delinquent
b. influence
c. brilliant
d. ingredient
e. consequently
f. science

89. Read each sentence and complete the spelling of each.

a. To neglect or fail to do is to be delin_____.

b. His mother has a lot of influ_____ on him.

c. Bob has been called a brilli_____ student.

d. The cook scolded the apprentice for leaving out an ingredi_____.

e. It is raining; consequ_____ly I won't go.

f. Nancy has won a scholarship in sci_____.

ence

90. Words having *flu* and *qu* have which ending (*ance, ence*)? _____

exceptions

91. Would the following words illustrate the usual tendency of *d* or are they exceptions? _____
abundance   attendance   guidance
descendant   defendant

no—it is an exception

92. Is the word *brilliant* a good example of the usual tendency of *i*? _____

ence

93. The consonants *l* and *n* tend to take which ending (*ance, ence*)? _____

ance   ance
ance

94. Complete the endings.
bal_____   domin_____
mainten_____

consist
persist
compet

95. The consonant *t* and *v* tend to take *ance*. The word *exist* is an exception, so is *insist*. Name the other three words (or bases) that are exceptions. _____
_____   _____

a. *ance*
b. *ance*
c. *ance*
d. *ance*

96. Choose the correct ending (*ance, ence*).

a. resist_____   c. import_____

b. relev_____   d. assist_____

g and c are hard
and require *ance*

97. State why *extravagance* and *significance* have *ance* and not *ence*.
_____

ence
each has a soft c
or g

98. Which ending (*ance, ence*) would you add to these words:
emerg_____   intellig_____   adolesc_____
magnific_____
State your reason briefly. _____
_____

a. defendant
b. guidance
c. abundance (ant)
d. descendant

99. From each twosome, choose one that takes *ance* or *ant*.

a. defend_____ depend_____

b. confid_____ guid_____

c. accid_____ abund_____

d. descend_____ anteced_____

POSTTEST

Supply the correct ending for each of the following.

A. *ary-ery*

1. contempor_____   5. Febru_____
2. station_____ (fixed)   6. secret_____
3. bound_____   7. libr_____
4. cemet_____   8. station_____ (paper)

B. *ise-ize-yze*

1. ar_____   7. adv_____
2. superv_____   8. exerc_____
3. character_____   9. critic_____
4. anal_____   10. paral_____
5. surpr_____   11. real_____
6. recogn_____   12. summar_____

C. *able-ible*

1. multipli_____   9. corrupt_____
2. enforce_____   10. revoc_____
3. perfect_____   11. kiss_____
4. enjoy_____   12. horr_____
5. admiss_____   13. consol_____
6. respons_____   14. irrit_____
7. commend_____   15. intellig_____
8. leg_____   16. dispens_____

D. ance-ence

1. sci_____ (*ence, ance*)
2. conveni_____ (*ence, ance*)
3. descend_____ (*ant, ent*)
4. import_____ (*ence, ance*)
5. domin_____ (*ence, ance*)
6. extravag_____ (*ent, ant*)
7. abund_____ (*ance, ence*)
8. resist_____ (*ance, ence*)
9. persist_____ (*ence, ance*)
10. attend_____ (*ance, ence*)
11. bal_____ (*ence, ance*)
12. adolesc_____ (*ent, ant*)
13. signific_____ (*ance, ence*)
14. delinqu_____ (*ent, ant*)
15. compet_____ (*ent, ant*)
16. defend_____ (*ant, ent*)
17. mainten_____ (*ance, ence*)
18. relev_____ (*ent, ant*)
19. excell_____ (*ence, ance*)
20. brilli_____ (*ant, ent*)
21. perman_____ (*ant, ent*)
22. guid_____ (*ance, ence*)
23. afflu_____ (*ant, ent*)
24. emerg_____ (*ence, ance*)

Part Two
MEANING
AND SPELLING

Chapter 7

THE "SEED" ROOTS

Because the roots *sede*, *cede*, and *ceed* are pronounced alike ("seed"), they must be distinguished by another means, their meaning. And so in this chapter you will concentrate on the meaning of these roots as well as on the meaning of various prefixes to be attached to these roots, and practice spelling a number of useful words. By the end of the chapter you will be combining the right prefix to the right root and understand the reasons for your choice. Also, by learning the meanings of the prefixes included in this chapter you will be able to choose the correct prefix for other words.

PRETEST

A. Fill in the blanks with the appropriate ending:

ceed, sede, cede

1. ac_____   5. ex_____   9. super_____

2. pro_____   6. suc_____   10. inter_____

3. con_____   7. ante_____

4. se_____   8. re_____

B. Fill in the appropriate prefix.

11. To replace is to _____sede.

12. To yield consent is to _____cede.

13. To advance is to _____ceed.

14. To go before is to _____cede.

15. To be successful is to _____ceed.

16. To settle differences is to ___cede.

17. To go beyond is to _____ceed.

18. To withdraw from a political group is to _____cede.

19. To yield strongly or to admit is to _____cede.

20. To go back is to _____cede.

1. Word endings that sound like "seed" are easy to learn as there are only three: *sede   cede   ceed*. The *sede* ending has only one prefix combined with it: *super*. The *ceed* ending has only three: *pro, ex, suc*. The *cede* ending takes other prefixes.
For the following prefixes attach the correct root.

a. con_____   e. ac_____

b. pro_____   f. ex_____

c. pre_____   g. inter_____

d. suc_____   h. super_____

a. cede   e. cede
b. ceed   f. ceed
c. cede   g. cede
d. ceed   h. sede

2. *Super* means over or above. Combining this prefix with the root that comes from the Latin *sedere*, meaning to sit, produces the word meaning that which sits above or over, in other words, replaces it. That word is _____.

supersede

3. How does this Latin verb *sedere* govern the spelling of the English derivative? _____

it has *sede* in it

4. The word that means to "sit over or above" or to replace is _____.

supersede

5. Three words have a different ending—*ceed*—which comes from the Latin *cedere*, meaning to go. The prefix *pro* means forward, *ex* means beyond, and *suc* (a variant of *sub*) means toward.
If one goes forward, he _____ceeds; if he goes beyond, he _____ceeds; if he goes toward (a goal, for example), he _____ceeds.

pro
ex
suc

6. Read the sentences for their meaning, then write the correct "seed" word for each.

a. Why can't the meeting _____?

b. Drew knew he was going to _____ the speed limit.

c. You must try hard if you want to _____.

d. The demand for strawberries will _____ the supply.

e. If you don't _____ at first, try again.

f. Now you can _____ with the second part of the examination.

a. proceed
b. exceed
c. succeed
d. exceed
e. succeed
f. proceed

7. What three words end in *ceed*?

_____   _____   _____

exceed   proceed
succeed

supersede

8. Name the only word ending in *sede.*

_____

cede

9. The rest of the "seed" words must end in (*sede, cede, ceed*). _____

cede

10. The third ending which also comes from the Latin *cedere,* meaning to go or to withdraw, constitutes a complete word, meaning to surrender possession formally, usually rights or territory. If a country formally gives up some of its possessions, it is said to _____ them.

cede

11. Some countries have been forced to _____ parts of their territories.

precede

12. Prefixes can be combined with this root to form quite a few words. For instance, adding *pre,* which means before, gives you the word _____.

before

13. If one precedes another, he goes _____ him.
before, after

precede

14. If you tell an anecdote before you begin your main speech, this anecdote will _____ the speech.

recede

15. Let us try another with the same root. The prefix *re* means back. To go back would be to _____.

recede

16. The tidal waters will _____ in about an hour.

precede
recede

17. To go before is to _____; to go back is to _____.

a. accede
b. concede

18. The prefix *ac* means to, so with this root it forms *accede,* meaning to go to, or to yield consent. *Con* in *concede* is an intensifier, so this word has a strong meaning of yielding (for example, a privilege or a right) or of admitting.
Write the appropriate word in each sentence.

a. The members of the minority party will eventually _____ to the wishes of the majority.

b. After a bitter conflict, the senator agreed to _____ to the chairman's demands.

concede

19. Which word has the stronger sense of yielding: *accede, concede?* _____

a. accede
b. concede

20. Read the sentences first to decide which has the stronger sense of yielding, then write the correct word.

a. Joe urged his brother to _____ to his parents' wishes.

b. I doubt that Don Hardy will ever _____ his voting rights.

a. 4
b. 2
c. 3
d. 5
e. 1

21. Now match these words with their definitions.

a. cede   1. to go before   _____

b. accede   2. to yield consent   _____

c. recede   3. to go back   _____

d. concede   4. to surrender   _____

e. precede   5. to yield a right   _____

a. cede   e. cede
b. ceed   f. cede
c. sede   g. ceed
d. ceed   h. cede

22. Complete these words.

a. ac_____   e. con_____

b. ex_____   f. pre_____

c. super_____   g. suc_____

d. pro_____   h. re_____

intercedes

23. *Inter* means between or among. If one goes between two persons, say to settle a quarrel, he inter_____.

antecedes

24. *Ante* means to precede in time or space. An event that goes before another in time _____ it.

antecedes

25. The First World War _____ the Second World War.

intercede

26. To act between parties to settle differences is to _____.

recede

27. The weather bureau predicted that the river would reach its crest and then would start to _____.

between

28. To intercede is to go _____.

a. ante
b. inter
c. pro
d. ex

29. Read the sentences for their meaning, then choose the correct prefix for each root: ac   pre   ante   inter   pro   ex   con

a. The period prior to the Civil War is called _____bellum.

b. Since the members have reached a deadlock, I hope that an arbitration board will _____cede soon.

c. Let us _____ceed with the meeting.

d. The supply will _____ceed the demand.

REVIEW

supersede

30. Write the word ending in *sede*. _____

exceed   proceed
succeed

31. What words end in *ceed*? _____

_____

a. *ceed*   f. *cede*
b. *cede*   g. *cede*
c. *sede*   h. *ceed*
d. *ceed*   i. *cede*
e. *cede*   j. *cede*

32. Finish the spelling.

a. suc_____   f. con_____

b. inter_____   g. pre_____

c. super_____   h. pro_____

d. ex_____   i. retro_____

e. ac_____   j. ante_____

secede

33. The Latin *se* meaning away or apart can be combined with the root that comes from the Latin *cedere*, meaning to go. If a state would "go away" from the Union it would _____ from the Union.

a. above
b. toward
c. away (apart)
d. back
e. beyond
f. before
g. forward
h. between

34. Supply the correct prefix meanings.

a. To supersede means to sit over or _____.

b. To succeed is to go _____ a goal.

c. To secede is to go _____.

d. To recede is to go _____.

e. To exceed is to go _____.

f. To precede is to go _____.

g. To proceed is to go _____.

h. To intercede is to act _____.

proceed
precede

35. The word meaning to go forward is _____; the word meaning to go before, or in front of, is _____.

a. precede
b. proceed
c. supersede

36. The following words are misspelled. Write the words correctly.

a. preceed   _____

b. procede   _____

c. supercede   _____

POSTTEST

A. Fill in the blanks with the appropriate "seed" ending.

1. re_____   5. ac_____   9. suc_____

2. ex_____   6. pro_____   10. ante_____

3. pre_____   7. super_____

4. con_____   8. se_____

B. Read the sentences carefully, then write the correct "seed" word for each.

11. When the road is cleared, the parade will _____ up the street.

12. The water will _____ by tomorrow.

13. John will _____ to the desires of his parents.

14. If Mary stands in front of Jack in the ticket line, she _____ him.

15. As the age of automation continues, new methods of production and management will _____ the old.
                  replace

16. If you are not careful, you will _____ the limit.

17. The teachers asked the superintendent to _____ in their dispute.
                                act between

18. To strongly yield consent is the definition of the word _____.

Chapter 8

HOMONYMS

Homonyms are words that sound exactly alike but differ in spelling and meaning. A spelling error occurs when one homonym is substituted for another. For instance, if you use *principle,* meaning a rule or law, for *principal,* meaning a head of a group, you will produce a confusing sentence, not only momentarily puzzling your reader, but undoubtedly irking him as well. The homonyms included in this chapter are those that cause a great deal of difficulty. But by the time you finish the chapter, you will have no difficulty with them. The main objective of this chapter is to provide you with sufficient material concerning the meanings and the parts of speech of these homonyms so that you can readily choose between them, not only according to their definitions but also in the context of sentences. Also, by working diligently with these homonyms, you can form a basis for learning other pairs (or sets) of words identical in sound.

PRETEST

Choose the correct homonyms for these sentences.

1. The president of the firm paid me a high _____.
   complement, compliment

2. I placed the book _____.
   their, there, they're

3. We are _____ too late.
   all ready, already

4. The dog wagged _____ tail.
   it's, its

5. Burlap is a _____ material.
   course, coarse

6. What is your _____ reason?
   principle, principal

7. The recommendation was made by the _____ members.
   council, counsel

8. He is _____ correct.
   all together, altogether

9. Did you buy any _____?
   stationery, stationary

10. I am meeting Judge Doe in his office at the state _____.
    capital, capitol

11. For your report you must _____ two references.
    sight, cite, site

12. He almost _____ directly in front of us.
    past, passed

13. Mary wants to go _____.
    to, too

14. The well is on _____ property.
    their, there

15. How far is the _____ for the new hospital from here?
    sight, site

16. It was a _____ performance!
    capitol, capital

---

a. already
b. all ready

1 Two expressions that are used interchangeably when they should not be are *all ready* and *already*. Besides being different in the number of words, they have different meanings. *All ready* is an adjective phrase meaning quite or completely ready. *Already* is an adverb meaning at or by this time.
Write the appropriate expression.

a. The best tickets were _____ sold.

b. We are _____ to go to the lake.

all ready
already

2. The expression meaning quite or completely ready is _____; the one meaning at or by this time is _____.

a. all ready
b. already

3. Choose the correct homonym: *all ready, already.*

a. By noon the soldiers were _____ to move to the front.

b. By the time we arrived, John had _____ gone.

2 2

4. The expression meaning completely or quite ready has how many words _____ and how many *l*'s _____?

1 1

5. The expression meaning at or by this time has how many words _____ and how many *l*'s _____?

all together
altogether

6. *All together* and *altogether* are another pair. The two-word expression concentrates on the *all*—everyone in a group—whereas the single word has meanings of completely, on the whole, or thoroughly. Which expression is correct for each sentence: After the storm the farmer found the animals huddled _____. I am _____ certain that he lied.

everyone in a group
on the whole,
completely,
thoroughly

7. Write the correct meaning(s) for each expression.

all together _____

altogether _____

a. altogether
b. altogether
c. all together

8. Choose the correct expression: *all together, altogether.*

a. The assumption is _____ false.

b. The critics said the performance was _____ entertaining.

c. To win a lasting peace, nations must work _____.

2

9. Here is a controversial pair: *all right* and *alright.* For some time the one-word expression has been considered (and still is by some) a misspelling of the two words, meaning satisfactory or correct. Today *alright* is accepted as an alternative form, but usually in informal writing only. The one way you can always be right is to spell this expression as _____ word(s).

informal

10. Alright is accepted by some but only in (formal, informal) writing. _____

all right

11. Which form is always correct? _____

all right

12. Choose the expression that is correct in all styles of writing:
His responses to the panel's inquiries were _____.

alright   all right

building

13. Although *capital* and *capitol* are easily confused, they are just as easy to use correctly. *Capitol* (with an o) is the building in which a state legislature meets, a building that usually has a dome on top. *Capitol* (with a capital C) refers to the building in Washington, D.C., where Congress meets. *Capital* (with an a) is used in contexts which demand other meanings than the _____ where a legislature assembles.

capitol
Capitol

14. The state legislature assembles at the _____ and the Congress of the U.S. occupies the _____ in Washington, D.C.

capital

15. If you remember that *capitol* relates to a building, then it is easy to use *capital* correctly for other meanings. For example, the major city or town of a state is called a _____ .

capital

16. Lima is the _____ of Peru.

capital

17. This word also has the meaning of first-rate or excellent: It was a _____ performance

capital

18. Or, the meaning of a stock of wealth. To buy the franchise, the grocer needed a great deal of _____ .

a. Capitol
   capital
b. capitol
   Capitol
   capital

19. Choose the correct one: *capital, Capitol, capitol*

a. To finance my trip to the _____ in Washton, D.C. I need more _____ .

b. When referring to the building where a state legislature meets you write _____ ; to the building where Congress meets _____ ; and to the major city of a state _____ .

a. principal
b. principal
c. principles
d. principal

20. The nouns *principle* and *principal* are easy to distinguish. *Principle* is a noun only and refers to basic truths, laws, or rules. *Principal* can be either an adjective meaning chief or main, or a noun referring to a leader, or a sum of money. Choose the correct homonym.

a. The head of a school is a _____ .

b. He cited three _____ reasons.

c. The community recognized him as a man of high _____ s.

d. A sum of money on which interest is calculated is _____ .

noun
wrong (incorrect)

21. The word principle is not correct in this phrase "a principle reason" because it can be used only as a _____, not as an adjective. Also the meaning is _____ for this context.

principle

22. The noun referring to basic truths, laws, or rules is _____.

a. principle
b. principal
principal
principles
c. principal

23. Choose the correct homonym: *principal, principle.*

a. Some people live only according to the _____ of self-preservation.

b. The _____ reason Mr. Brown was appointed _____ of Stock High School is that he has high _____.

c. Mr. Raymond's account totaled $1,000, of which approximately $900 was the _____.

a. stationary
b. stationery

24. *Stationery* and *stationary* are another good pair to learn. *Stationery* is a noun, meaning either the paper you write on or the establishment that sells it and related items. *Stationary* is an adjective meaning fixed, not movable. Write the appropriate word.

a. He remained _____.

b. My mother bought me some _____.

stationary
stationery

25. The adjective meaning fixed is _____; the noun meaning writing paper is _____.

stationery

26. The last syllable of the word *paper* contains *er,* and so does the last syllable of the word for writing paper: _____.

noun

27. In this sentence—The architect suggested putting in stationary seats—the word *stationery* cannot be substituted because the sentence needs the adjective to modify seats, and *stationery* is always a _____.

stationery

28. Mavis wrote to me on her best _____.

stationary

29. The rows of seats in the auditorium are _____.

a. coarse
b. course
c. coarse
d. course
e. course

30. The adjective *coarse* cannot be substituted for the noun *course*. *Coarse*, meaning inferior in quality, crude, or harsh, is always an adjective. *Course*, on the other hand, can be used as a noun or verb, but never as an adjective. As a noun, it means a direction, route, or onward movement; as a verb it means to follow a direction.
Supply the correct word.

a. Burlap is a _____ material.

b. He follows a definite _____.

c. She has _____ manners.

d. We followed the _____ of the stream.

e. Rivers _____.

coarse

31. Although his manners were _____, he had an engaging personality.

course

32. Fads usually run their _____ in a short time.
course, coarse

coarse
course
verb

33. Whereas _____ is always an adjective, _____ is either a noun or a _____.

a. site
b. sight
c. cite
d. sight
e. sight

34. *Site, cite,* and *sight* are homonyms to watch out for. *Site* is always a noun and means a place of location or an event. *Cite* is always a verb, meaning to mention or quote as an authority. *Sight* can be used as a noun or a verb. As a noun it can mean one's vision, a field of vision, or a spectacle.
Choose the correct homonym.

a. Orchard Gardens is the _____ for a new development project.

b. Soon the sailor will _____ land.

c. The politician will _____ many authorities to back up his claims.

d. He should _____ his target at any minute.

e. Suddenly it came into _____.

site
noun
cite
verb
noun
sight

35. The word meaning a place of location _____ is always a _____.
noun, verb
The word meaning to mention or quote an authority _____ is always a _____.
The third homonym can mean to take aim, as a verb, or a view or spectacle as a _____. This word is _____.

a. cite
b. sight
c. site
d. sighted

36. Choose one for these sentences: *cite site sight*

a. Did you _____ Forster's theory?

b. The Grand Canyon is a breathtaking _____.

c. We came around the curve and then saw the _____ for the plant.

d. He raised his rifle and carefully _____ his target.

REVIEW

a. capitol
b. course
c. all ready
d. stationery
e. principal
f. cite
g. altogether
h. already
i. site
j. coarse

37. Now test your skill by writing the correct homonyms.

a. I drove to the _____ in twenty minutes.
                          state legislature building

b. Richard has decided on a definite _____ of
                                              coarse, course
action.

c. When the whistle blew, the workers were _____
                                                  already, all ready
to leave.

d. Jane received two boxes of _____.
                                    stationary, stationery

e. The speaker emphasized the _____
                                     principal, principle
points strongly.

f. He did not _____ sufficient evidence to
                  site, cite, sight
win.

g. Her behavior is _____ proper.
                        altogether, all together

h. By the time Joe arrived, his brother had _____
                                                  all ready, already
_____ left.

i. My uncle picked a _____ in the country for
                          sight, site
his new house.

j. The lady chose a _____ material for her
                         course, coarse
drapes.

a. P e. P
b. C f. C
c. P g. P
d. C h. C

38. Contractions are not to be mistaken for possessives. Contractions are identified by an apostrophe which stands for an omitted letter. For example, the ' in *it's* stands for the omitted *i* in the verb: it *is*. The possessive *its* never has an apostrophe. Identify by P or C whether these words are possessives or contractions.

a. their _____   e. whose _____

b. who's _____   f. it's _____

c. its _____   g. your _____

d. you're _____   h. they're _____

who *is*
it *is*
you *are*
they *are*

39. In the contractions the apostrophe stands for the beginning letter of a verb. What is it in *who's?* _____ in *it's?* _____ in *you're?* _____ in *they're?* _____

a. who's
b. you're
c. its
d. their

40. Choose the correct words.

a. Do you know _____ going to the dance?
who's, whose

b. Tell me when _____ ready.
your, you're

c. We watched the mother bird feed _____ young.
it's, its

d. They did not like _____ seats downstairs.
they're, their

They're
there
their

41. A word sounding exactly like *their* and *they're* is *there*. It is an adverb meaning in or at that place: I placed the package over *there*. Write the correct word—*there, their, they're*, in these related sentences.
Nancy shouted, "_____ here."
"Where?" I replied. "Over _____," she said, "waving _____ hands."

a. too
b. two
c. to
d. to
e. too

42. These words also sound alike but differ in meaning and spelling: *to too two*. The word *two* pertains to the number 2. *To* (with one o) can be a preposition, as in *to the store*, or it can help to form an infinitive, as in *to go* home. *Too* (with two o's) is an adverb meaning also or more than enough: I want to go *too*, or It is *too* much.
Fill in the correct homonyms below.

a. Do you want a cone _____?

b. I received a _____ dollar raise.

c. Mary went downtown _____ buy a robe.

d. Don't bother about giving a present _____ me.

e. There is _____ much noise.

two
too
to

43. The numeral is _____; the adverb is _____; the proposition or part of an infinitive is _____.

a. too
b. two
c. to
d. too

44. Choose the correct homonym: *to, too, two.*

a. I, _____, was offered a job there.

b. The typist gets _____ dollars an hour.

c. Don't give it _____ her.

d. We had _____ many problems to worry about Jim's ball game.

verb

45. You need never confuse *know* and *no* because *know* is a verb meaning to perceive, or to be certain of, and *no* is either an adjective "no bananas are left," or an adverb, "he is no better than I."
In this sentence—How do you know he is over twenty—you cannot use *no* because it is an adverb or an adjective, and the sentence requires a _____.

a. know
b. no
c. no
d. know

46. Write *know* or *no* below.

a. I don't _____ the instructor.

b. He is _____ better than he appears to be.

c. I looked, but there were _____ strawberries on the counter.

d. How do you _____ he is right?

no   know

47. The word that means none as an adjective and not as an adverb is _____. The word that sounds like it but is a verb is _____.

passed—sentence
needs a verb

48. *Passed* and *past* should present no problem as *passed* is simply the past tense (*ed*) of the verb *pass:* He passed in front of me. *Past* can be either a noun: a distinguished *past,* an adjective: in *past* years, or an adverb: walked *past* the store. In this sentence—He _____ me on the street—which homonym is correct and why?

past

49. Of the two, *passed* and *past,* which one can be either a noun, adjective, or adverb? _____

a. passed
b. past
c. past
passed

50. Write *passed* or *past* for these sentences.

a. The train _____ within 20 feet.

b. He thanked us for _____ favors.

c. In the _____ the Johnsons have _____ us on the street without any sign of recognition.

---

a. yes
b. meaning is wrong
—need verb meaning
praise

51. Although both *compliment* and *complement* are nouns and verbs, they have such different meanings that they should never be confused. A *compliment* is an expression of praise, and *to compliment* is to praise someone. A *complement* is something that completes and *to complement* is to complete.

a. Is the homonym used correctly in this sentence: The new complement of soldiers arrived today. _____

b. Why won't *complement* fit this sentence: He continued to compliment me for my fine work. _____

---

a. compliment
compliment
b. complemented
c. complement
complimented

52. Write in *complement* or *compliment*.

a. I waited for him to _____ me, but when the _____ came, it dripped with sarcasm.

b. In finishing the design, Mrs. White _____ the rows of red figures with a row of blue ones.

c. When the fresh _____ of soldiers arrived, the general _____ them on their appearance.

---

a. council is a noun,
it means a group
b. yes
c. counsel

53. The last group is *council, counsel,* and *consul.* All three are nouns. A *council* is a deliberative body (like a city council, for example). *Counsel* means either a lawyer or a group of lawyers giving advice, or the advice itself. *Consul* refers to an officer in the foreign service of his country. *Counsel* can also be a verb, to give advice or to recommend.

a. In this sentence—He tried to _____ me about going to college—*council* would be incorrect. State two reasons why. _____

b. Is the correct homonym used here: He offered his counsel. _____

c. Whereas *council* and *consul* are nouns only, _____ can be either a noun or a verb.

a. council
counsel
consul
b. council counsel
consul

54. Choose the correct word: *counsel, council, consul.*

a. A deliberative assembly is a _____; a lawyer who conducts a case in court is called _____; and an officer in the foreign service is a _____.

b. The student _____ sought _____ from the French _____.

counsel

55. Which word is not only a noun? _____

REVIEW

a. counsel
b. complement
c. their
d. to
e. its
f. passed
g. know no
h. You're
i. too
j. Who's
k. compliments

56. Test your skill in choosing the correct homonym.

a. My adviser tried to _____ me about enter-
    council, counsel
ing the contest.

b. The new _____ of soldiers saved
    compliment, complement
the fortress.

c. The couple insisted that we were going to camp on
_____ property.
    there, their

d. He decided not to give the money _____ the
    to, two, too
church.

e. Minnesota is known for _____ lakes.
    it's, its

f. As we neared the reviewing stand, Mike _____
    past, passed
us on the left.

g. Many inhabitants _____ _____ other way
    know, no   know, no
of life.

h. Jim gasped, "_____ going."
    Your, You're

i. I want to go _____.
    two, to, too

j. _____ driving to school?
    Whose, Who's

k. Lorraine received many _____
    compliments, complements
for her fine portrayal of Anna.

POSTTEST

Write the correct homony for each sentence.

1. The ruler suggested that a new _____ of militia be added.
   compliment, complement

2. Don't you know _____ meaning?
   it's, its

3. He has a distinguished _____.
   past, passed

4. Do you plan to take a specific _____?
   coarse, course

5. They huddled _____ in the barn.
   altogether, all together

6. How are you going to _____ him?
   council, counsel

7. It was a thrilling _____.
   cite, sight, site

8. The auditorium seats are _____.
   stationery, stationary

9. My uncle works at the _____ in Washington, D.C.
   capitol, capital, Capitol

10. Please give the dress _____ Doris.
    to, two, too

11. By the time we arrived he had _____ gone.
    all ready, already

12. The mother bird fed _____ young.
    its, it's

13. A foreign service officer is a _____.
    counsel, consul

14. _____ not going to the picnic.
    Their, There, They're

15. _____ magazine is this?
    Whose, Who's

16. The officer is a man of high _____.
    principal, principle

Chapter 9

SIMILAR WORDS

Words that are similar in appearance or sound can also be confused. For example, the pairs, *accept-except*, and *affect-effect*, are used interchangeably when they should not be. By noting differences in spelling, sound, and particularly meaning, you can quickly eliminate any hesitation in choosing the right word of such a pair, or set, as the case may be. The objectives of this chapter are therefore these: you will distinguish between alternatives by their meaning and spelling; you will practice spelling and using a number of these similar words, and you will establish a *modus operandi* for spelling other confusing words.

PRETEST

Choose the correct word for each sentence.

1. This has been _____ a day.
   quite, quiet

2. Do you have _____ to the storeroom?
   excess, access

3. I'm afraid I will _____ my place in line.
   loose, lose

4. His remarks were _____.
   causal, casual

5. Can you _____ what will happen?
   prophecy, prophesy

6. Please _____ my apologies.
   except, accept

7. He is taller _____ I.
   then, than

8. Do you expect any bad _____ from the new drug?
   affects, effects

9. Do a _____ job.
   through, thorough

10. Can you _____ the storm?
    whether, weather

11. I listened patiently to the complaints of the _____.
    personal, personnel

12. He cannot _____ me.
    advice, advise

13. Lucy tripped on the _____ floor board.
    lose, loose

---

a. access
b. excess
c. access

1. Access is a noun meaning a way of approaching or a right to enter. *Excess*, also a noun, means the act of going beyond, or exceeding. Since both words are nouns you must choose according to the meaning. Which one is correct in these sentences?

a. He has _____ to the vault.

b. There is an _____ of potatoes.

c. We have direct _____ to the stage.

access
excess

2. The word signifying a means of nearing is _____;
the word meaning the act of going beyond is _____.

a. excess
b. access
c. access

3. Choose the correct word: *access, excess.*

a. What shall we do about the _____ of basketballs?

b. How do you gain _____ to the wing of the building?

c. Because the boy's parents did not accompany him, he was refused _____.

way of nearing
act of going beyond

4. Access means _____.
Excess means _____.

No. Causal pertains to a cause. Sentence demands "unconcerned."

5. In the two adjectives *casual* and *causal* watch the placement of the s and u. The word that pertains to a cause would be *causal*; the word that means occurring by change, aimless, or unconcerned is *casual*. Is the underlined word used correctly here? If not, why not?
He has a <u>causal</u> appearance.

_____
_____

causal	**6.** The adjective that refers to a cause is _____.
a. casual b. causal casual c. casual	**7.** Choose the correct word: *casual, causal.* a. He has a _____ manner. b. To prove his argument he must show _____ relationships, not _____ ones. c. Because he had no time for preparation, he could offer only some _____ remarks.
unconcerned relating to a cause	**8.** Define *casual:* _____ Define *causal:* _____
yes in each case	**9.** *Affect* is a verb meaning to change or to alter. It is never a noun. *Effect,* on the other hand, is both a noun and a verb. As a noun it means a result; as a verb to bring about a result, or to accomplish. Are the underlined words used correctly in these sentences? a. What will the effect be? b. How do the legislators expect to effect the changes in the new law? c. The car accident affected his hearing.
affect effect	**10.** The verb meaning to change or alter is _____. The verb meaning to accomplish or bring about a result is _____.
a. affect b. effects c. effect	**11.** Choose the correct word: *affect, effect.* a. The new housing bill will _____ many people. b. What major _____s do you expect? c. Can the school system _____ the changes without more money?
verb alter, change result bring about a result, accomplish	**12.** *Affect* is always a _____ and means to _____. *Effect* as a noun means _____; as a verb it means _____.
prophecy	**13.** *Prophecy* and *prophesy* are easy to distinguish. First, *prophecy* is the noun and *prophesy* is the verb. Second, *to prophesy* is to predict, and what is predicted is the *prophecy.* Which word is correct for this sentence: He stated that his _____ would come true.

prophesy

14. Which word is the verb: *prophecy* or *prophesy?*

_____

prophecies

prophesy

15. All were astounded by her _____.

prophesies, prophecies

16. He demanded time to _____ but he was refused.

to predict
the prediction

17. Prophesy means _____.
Prophecy means _____.

a. Yes
b. Yes

18. The verb *accept* means to receive, to take willingly. It should not be confused with *except*, meaning other than or with the exclusion of. Check whether the underlined word is correct.

a. Everyone <u>except</u> Joe went home.
Yes _____ No _____

b. We will <u>accept</u> the offer.
Yes _____ No _____

receive
other than, with the
exclusion of

19. *Accept* means _____.
Except means _____.

a. except
b. accepts
c. except

20. Choose the correct word: *except, accept.*

a. All the bottles _____ one broke.

b. Everyone _____ s Grandma Smith as his friend.

c. All went to the picnic _____ Mac.

advise (the verb)

21. *Advise* (with an *s*) is a verb meaning to counsel; *advice* (with a *c*) is a noun meaning the counsel given. Which word is appropriate here:
What did he _____ you to do?

advise
advice

22. The counselor offered to _____ the students,

advise, advice

but he knew they would not accept his _____.

advice, advise

advise
advice

23. The verb meaning to counsel is _____; the noun meaning the counsel given is _____.

to counsel
the counsel given

24. *Advise* means _____.
Advice means _____.

(1) Sentence needs a verb. (2) Loose has the wrong meaning—context demands meaning of mislay.

25. *Lose* and *loose* differ in three ways. *Lose* is a verb; *loose* is an adjective. *Lose* means to mislay, to be deprived of; *loose* means free, not fastened down tight. *Lose* has one o; *loose* has two.
Name two reasons why *loose* cannot be used in this sentence: I always lose my gloves.

_____

_____

a. loose
b. lose
c. lose
d. lose

26. Select the correct word: *lose, loose.*

a. The bolt is _____.

b. If Tim is not careful, he will _____ his cap.

c. Don't _____ your balance.

d. So that you will not _____ any more time, take the bus.

adjective—free
verb—to mislay

27. *Loose* is an _____, meaning _____.
Lose is a _____, meaning _____.

quite quiet

28. *Quite* and *quiet* differ in spelling, meaning, and pronunciation. *Quite* has one syllable; *quiet* has two. *Quite* is an adverb meaning rather, actually, or completely. *Quiet* is an adjective meaning silent, away from noise. Combine these two words into a phrase meaning rather still:

_____

quite

29. Today is _____ hot for June.
         quiet, quite

cold

30. Since *quite* is an adverb, it modifies what word in this sentence: It is quite cold. _____

quiet

31. After ten o'clock the park is _____.

adjective
silent
adverb
rather, completely, actually

32. *Quiet* is an _____ and means _____.
Quite is an _____ and means _____.

REVIEW

a. advice
b. effects
c. prophecy
d. lose

33. Test your skill by selecting the correct words.

a. Whose _____ will you take?
         advice, advise

e. affect
f. quiet
g. accepted
h. access
i. causal

b. Don't expect too many good _____ from
   affects, effects

the new bill.

c. Many a _____ has come true.
   prophecy, prophesy

d. If you say yes, you may _____ your privileges.
   lose, loose

e. Jack's actions will _____ all of us.
   affect, effect

f. There is a _____ zone around the hospital.
   quite, quiet

g. His defeat was _____ good-naturedly.
   accepted, excepted

h. The corridor offers good _____ to all the
   excess, access

music studios.

i. He lost his argument by stating false _____
   casual, causal

relationships.

a. than
b. then

34. *Then* means at that time in the past: I was six then; or next in time or space: I will go to the store; then I will go downtown. *Than* relates to a statement showing comparison: Mary is more agile than Betty; or a preference: I would rather dance than eat.
Write the correct word for each sentence.

a. He is younger _____ I am.

b. He was younger _____.

then refers to time and space—than refers to a preference

35. In this sentence—I would rather dance than play golf—why can't you use *then?* _____

time and space
a comparison, a preference

36. The adverb *then* refers to _____.
The conjunction *than* refers to a _____
or a _____.

a. than
b. then
c. than

37. Choose the correct word: *then, than.*

a. He writes better _____ I do.

b. If she practices hard for the next half hour, _____ she can play outdoors.

c. I would prefer exercising on the machine rather _____ jogging for ten minutes.

a. through
b. thorough
c. through

38. *Through* and *thorough* are like *quite* and *quiet* in that one word has one syllable and the other two. *Through,* the one-syllable word, is a preposition which means by way of, to the end, to finish successfully. *Thorough,* the two-syllable word, is an adjective meaning complete, or painstakingly accurate.
Write the correct word for each sentence.

a. I got my information _____ Jane.

b. He did a _____ job.

c. I saw the performance _____.

thorough
through

39. The adjective meaning finished and accurate is _____. The preposition meaning by way of, to the end, or finish successfully is _____.

a. to the end
b. by way of
c. finish successfully

40. What is the meaning of *through* in these sentences?

a. The critic saw the opera through. _____

b. It was through John that we found out. _____

c. I got through the examination. _____

a. painstakingly accurate
b. complete

41. What does *thorough* mean here?

a. Josie is a thorough worker. _____

b. He listened with thorough enjoyment. _____

personnel

42. Now take *personal* and *personnel. Personal* is an adjective and pertains to something done to or for a person. *Personnel* is a noun referring to a body of persons employed or active in an organization. Which word is correct here?

The supervisor spoke to the _____.

personal
personnel

43. The adjective referring to a person is _____; the noun referring to people employed at an office is

_____.

a. personal
b. personnel
c. personal
d. personnel

44. Choose the correct word: *personal, personnel.*

a. He resigned for _____ reasons.

b. The factory _____ want a representative to discuss their needs.

c. After hearing the cases, the judge said that most of the complaints were _____.

d. The adjective *personal* cannot be substituted for the noun _____.

a person
a body of persons
at a company

45. *Personal* refers to _____.
Personnel refers to _____.

a. weather
b. whether
c. weather

46. Although *weather* and *whether* sound almost alike, they differ in all other respects. *Weather* is a noun that means atmospheric conditions, or a verb that means to expose to these conditions or to pass through an ordeal safely. *Whether* is a conjunction which introduces the first of two or more alternatives. Choose the correct word for each sentence.

a. We will have cold _____ soon.

b. It does not matter _____ we sit or stand.

c. I cannot _____ many more snowstorms.

whether

47. The word that introduces an alternative is (*weather, whether*). _____

verb

48. *Whether* is a conjunction, but *weather* serves either as a noun or as a _____.

whether
weather

49. The result of the debate matters not; what is important is _____ Tony can _____
              whether, weather   whether, weather
the long and tiring ordeal.

REVIEW

a. through
b. personnel
c. weather
d. than
e. whether
f. then

50. Choose the correct word for each sentence.

a. When you are _____ with the pamph-
              thorough, through
let, return it to me.

b. The administrator spoke to all the _____.
              personal, personnel

c. The forecast for tomorrow's _____ is
              weather, whether
rain.

d. Mr. Park owns more property _____ Mr. Stone.
              then, than

e. Don't ask me _____ I can go or not.
              whether, weather

f. Complete this assignment; _____ do the next.
              then, than

POSTTEST

Write the correct word(s) for each sentence.

1. You cannot make noise in the _____ zone.
   quite, quiet

2. We must know _____ the school is open.
   whether, weather

3. Please do me a _____ favor.
   personal, personnel

4. I hope the _____ boards have been fixed.
   lose, loose

5. The supply of ironing boards is in _____ of those needed.
   excess, access

6. To win your argument you must show _____ relationships.
   casual, causal

7. Everyone _____ Larry as a friend.
   accepts, excepts

8. We don't know what the _____ of his speech will be.
   effects, affects

9. The _____ came true.
   prophesy, prophecy

10. There are times when legislation is the only way to _____ the
    affect, effect
necessary changes.

11. When you finish this chapter, _____ begin the next.
    then, than

12. It's a question _____ I would rather dine out or stay home.
    weather, whether

13. What _____ will you give him tomorrow?
    advise, advice

Part Three
RULES
AND SPELLING

Chapter 10

DOUBLING THE FINAL CONSONANT

Knowing when to double the final consonant and when not to will help you to spell many words correctly. In this chapter you will not only learn several rules about doubling in words of one or more syllables, but you will also apply them to many words. Also you will learn to immediately recognize words that do not follow the doubling rule, words that do and do not double depending on the shift in stress when a suffix is added, and a few exceptions to the rules. By the end of the chapter you will not be misspelling *occurrence*, *transferring*, or other words requiring the final consonant to be doubled, nor will you be misspelling words that do not double the final consonant.

PRETEST

Add the specified suffixes to the following words.

1.	plan	er	_____	14.	gossip	y	_____
2.	wit	y	_____	15.	instill	ing	_____
3.	streak	ed	_____	16.	equip	ed	_____
4.	plug	er	_____	17.	omit	ed	_____
5.	tax	ing	_____	18.	dim	er	_____
6.	exploit	er	_____	19.	excel	ent	_____
7.	drop	ed	_____	20.	confer	ence	_____
8.	begin	ing	_____	21.	benefit	ed	_____
9.	occur	ence	_____	22.	chagrin	ed	_____
10.	dim	ly	_____	23.	vex	ing	_____
11.	repeal	ed	_____	24.	delight	ful	_____
12.	transfer	ing	_____	25.	traffic	er	_____
13.	propel	ant	_____				

c. d. f. g. h.
· · · · · · · · · · · · · ·
b. c. e. f. h.

1. One-syllable words ending in a single consonant preceded by a single vowel double the final consonant before adding a suffix beginning with a vowel (or the suffix *y*). For instance, the word *cup* ends in a single consonant (*p*) preceded by a single vowel (*u*). If you add the suffix *ed* (which begins with the vowel *e*) you double the consonant: *cupped.* But if you add the suffix *ful* (which begins with the consonant *f*) you do not double the *p*: *cupful.* Let us look at the words *link* and *peel. Link* ends in two consonants (*nk*) and *peel* in a consonant preceded by two vowels (*eel*), so these words do not meet the requirements.

One consonant cannot be doubled even though it is preceded by a vowel. This consonant—*x*—has a *ks* sound and is treated as two consonants. Take the word *tax* as an example; pronounce it slowly and you will hear the *ks* sound. If you add *ed* to tax you would spell it: *taxed.*

In the one-syllable words below identify those that end in a single consonant preceded by a single vowel.

a. hail	d. club	g. bug
b. drill	e. pack	h. rip
c. mop	f. tap	

· ·

Identify the suffixes that would require doubling.

a. *ment*	d. *ly*	g. *ful*
b. *ing*	e. *y*	h. *ance*
c. *er*	f. *ed*	

a. chatty
e. dimmed
f. clammy
g. fretting

2. Pick out each combination of a word and a suffix to which this doubling rule applies, add the specified suffix, and write the complete word. If the rule does not apply to a combination, leave the space blank.

a. chat	*y*	_____
b. streak	*ed*	_____
c. farm	*er*	_____
d. tax	*ing*	_____
e. dim	*ed*	_____
f. clam	*y*	_____
g. fret	*ing*	_____
h. burn	*er*	_____

b. stooped
d. fretful
e. taxed
f. pealing
h. grimly

3. If a particular word or suffix does not meet the requirements of this rule, you can assume that the final consonant is not doubled before the suffix. Choose the combinations below to which this rule does *not* apply, add the
specified suffix, and write the complete words.

a. bar   *ed*   _____

b. stoop   *ed*   _____

c. stop   *ed*   _____

d. fret   *ful*   _____

e. tax   *ed*   _____

f. peal   *ing*   _____

g. chub   *y*   _____

h. grim   *ly*   _____

a. planner
b. droplet
c. restful
d. clubs
e. dimmer
f. speared
g. shrieking
h. plugged
i. skinny
j. dimly
k. vexing
l. dropped

4. Now test your skill by writing complete words for all
the combinations.

a. plan   *er*   _____

b. drop   *let*   _____

c. rest   *ful*   _____

d. club   *s*   _____

e. dim   *er*   _____

f. spear   *ed*   _____

g. shriek   *ing*   _____

h. plug   *ed*   _____

i. skin   *y*   _____

j. dim   *ly*   _____

k. vex   *ing*   _____

l. drop   *ed*   _____

REVIEW

c. d. f.

5. Which factors must be considered in the doubling of
the final consonant in a one-syllable word?

a. it must end in a single vowel

b. it must end in a single consonant preceded by a single
consonant

c. it must end in a single consonant preceded by a single
vowel

d. it must not end in the consonant *x*

e. the suffix begins with a consonant

f. the suffix begins with a vowel or is the suffix *y*

last *f* is preceded by another *f* (consonant)

6. Why don't you double the final consonant in *puff?*
_____

the *k* is preceded by two vowels (*oa*)

7. In adding the suffix *ed* to *soak*, the *k* is not doubled. Why not? _____

the suffix *ly* begins with a consonant (*l*)

8. Even though *dim* ends in a single consonant preceded by a single vowel, you do not double the *m* before *ly*. Why not? _____

a. cupful
b. stopper
c. shrouded
d. mopped
e. witty
f. taxing
g. primly
h. pouter
i. tags
j. deepest
k. pithy
l. kindness

9. Test your skill by adding the suffixes to these one-syllable words.

a. cup   *ful*   _____

b. stop   *er*   _____

c. shroud   *ed*   _____

d. mop   *ed*   _____

e. wit   *y*   _____

f. tax   *ing*   _____

g. prim   *ly*   _____

h. pout   *er*   _____

i. tag   *s*   _____

j. deep   *est*   _____

k. pith   *y*   _____

l. kind   *ness*   _____

10. Words of more than one syllable must also have a single consonant preceded by a single vowel to be doubled. Also, the stress (or accent) must be on the *last* syllable. Take the word *compel.* It ends in *l* preceded by *e*, and the stress is on the last syllable. Since it meets all the requirements, the *l* is doubled before a suffix beginning with a vowel: *compel* + *ed* = *compelled.* If a word does not meet these requirements, then the final consonant is not doubled. Take the verbs *instill* and *exploit.* Although the accent is on the last syllable in each, the *l* is preceded by another *l* and the *t* is preceded by two vowels. The final consonant *x* is the exception here as well, as the *x* (pronounced like *ks*) counts as two consonants. Even though the word *relax* meets the requirements, the *x* is not doubled.

Now identify those words that have the stress on the last syllable:

a. recur   d. prefer

b. offer   e. enter

c. differ   f. propel

• •

Look at and pronounce each word, then match it with the correct explanation for doubling or not doubling.

a. enchant   _____   e. compel   _____

b. occur   _____   f. repeal   _____

c. benefit   _____   g. determine _____

d. enlighten _____

1. doubles: accent and ending correct
2. does not double: ending correct, but accent is wrong
3. does not double: accent and ending are wrong
4. does not double: accent correct but ending is wrong

11. Applying the doubling rule when appropriate, add the specified suffixes to the following words.

a. refer   *ed*   _____

b. visit   *or*   _____

c. benefit   *ed*   _____

d. repel   *ent*   _____

e. rebut   *al*   _____

f. repeal   *ing*   _____

g. occur   *ence*   _____

h. gossip   *y*   _____

12. *Equip* ends in a single consonant preceded by two vowels *u* and *i*. However, only the *i* counts as a vowel because a *u* combined with a *q* makes a *kw* sound (e kwip). *Equip* then meets the requirements of this rule.

There is one suffix *age* before which you do not double the *p*.

Choose the suffixes before which you would double the *p* in *equip*.

a. *ing*   c. *ed*

b. *ment*   d. *age*

equipped equipage
equipment
equipping

13. Add the following suffixes to equip:

ed _____   *age* _____

ment _____   *ing* _____

transferring
transferred

14. Modern usage permits two pronunciations of *transfer:* tran̉sfer or transfeŕ. In spelling the word, however, you follow the doubling rule. Add *ing* and *ed* to this word.

_____   _____

a. controlling
b. occurred
c. equipped
d. difference
e. beginning
f. transferred
g. happened
h. revealed
i. appearance
j. benefited
k. recurring
l. patrolling
m. relaxing

15. Now combine the root word and suffix for each sentence.

a. The nurse had a difficult time _____ the
                                         control *ing*
patient.

b. This same situation has _____ many times.
                                occur *ed*

c. The kitchen was _____ with the latest ap-
                        equip *ed*
pliances.

d. Many cannot see the _____ between the two
                            differ *ence*
items.

e. Since I lost my place, I will have to start reading from
the _____.
        begin *ing*

f. My father has been _____ to Detroit.
                           transfer *ed*

g. What has _____ to the Olsons?
                happen *ed*

h. A thorough study of the project _____ several
                                        reveal *ed*
statistical errors.

i. The prima donna has made only one concert
_____ this year.
    appear *ance*

j. Many peasants have _____ from the agrarian
                           benefit *ed*
reform program.

k. The invalid was plagued by a _____ fever.
                                     recur *ing*

l. The municipal police department does a good job of
_____ the area.
    patrol *ing*

m. Fishing can be a _____ sport.
                        relax *ing*

The *l* was doubled before the suffix, so the extra *l* must be taken off to form the original word

a. control
b. excel
c. repel
d. compel

16. Sometimes the word that requires doubling is misspelled. Take *rebellion,* for example. The word is made up of two parts, the root and the suffix. Take away the suffix *ion* and you have "rebell." This is the wrong spelling of the root. Why? _____

17. Now reduce these words to their roots.

a. controlled _____

b. excellent _____

c. repelling _____

d. compeller _____

chagrined

18. The word *chagrin,* which means mental distress, ends in a single consonant preceded by a single vowel and the stress is on the last syllable. But it is an exception to the doubling rule. Add the suffix *ed* to this word. _____

chagrin

19. The word which means mental distress is an exception to the doubling rule. That word is _____.

chagrin

20. If a person is suffering from embarrassment or distress caused by failure he is suffering from _____.

last
first
second *r*

21. If the addition of a suffix causes the stress to be shifted to an earlier syllable, then the final consonant is not doubled. Let us add *ed* and then *ence* to occur: *occurred* and *occurrence.* There has been no shift in accent as it is still on occuṙ. Now add *ed* and *ence* to *refer.* On what syllable is the stress in *referred* (first, last)? _____ in *reference* (first, last)? _____ What letter is missing in the second word? _____

yes

22. In your mind add *ence* to these words: *prefer, confer, infer, defer.* Are these examples of words in which the accent shifts to an earlier syllable? _____

excellent   excellence

23. Now pronounce these words: *excelled excelling excellent excellence.* The root word is *excel,* which has the stress on the last syllable. In which of the above words, if any, does the accent shift? _____

no

24. Do *excellent* and *excellence* follow the same spelling pattern as *reference?* _____

double

25. *Excel* is then an exception. Regardless of the shift in stress to an earlier syllable, you still _____ the final *l*.

excel

26. What is the root of *excellent* or *excelling*? _____

27. Pronounce the following complete words carefully. Then write them.

a. conference
b. referred
c. excellent
d. preference
e. conferred
f. deferring
g. reference
h. excelled

a. confer   *ence*   _____

b. refer   *ed*   _____

c. excel   *ent*   _____

d. prefer   *ence*   _____

e. confer   *ed*   _____

f. defer   *ing*   _____

g. refer   *ence*   _____

h. excel   *ed*   _____

yes
yes
no

28. The last few words to be studied also end in a single consonant preceded by a single vowel (*ic*). But the stress is not on the last syllable, so the final *c* is not doubled. There is a pronunciation problem, however, and these words must be treated for it. Take the word *picnic*. The final *c* has a hard sound (as in *cat*), not a soft sound (as in *city*), and to preserve this hard sound you must add a *k* before a suffix beginning with a vowel (or the suffix *y*). You do *not* need the *k* if the suffix begins with a consonant, like *ry* or *some*.
Pronounce these words: *traffic panic colic mimic*
Does the final *c* have a hard sound? _____
Is the *k* necessary before a vowel suffix? _____
Is the *k* necessary before a consonant suffix? _____

a. panicked
b. trafficker
c. frolicsome
d. colicky
e. mimicry
f. mimicking

29. Add the specified suffixes to these "ic" words.

a. panic   *ed*   _____   d. colic   *y*   _____

b. traffic *er*   _____   e. mimic   *ry*   _____

c. frolic   *some*   _____   f. mimic   *ing*   _____

REVIEW

a. e. g. h.

30. In general, what factors must be present to double the final consonant of a word having more than one syllable?

a. a suffix beginning with a vowel (or the suffix *y*)

b. a suffix beginning with a consonant

c. the final consonant is preceded by one or more vowels

d. the final consonant is preceded by one or more consonants

e. the final consonant is preceded by a single vowel

f. the accent can be on any syllable

g. the accent is on the last syllable

h. the consonant *x* is not doubled

a. shifts
b. excel
c. chagrin

31. The exceptions to this rule are

a. you do not double if the accent _____ back to an earlier syllable

b. one word doubles regardless of a shift in stress—it is

_____

c. the word meaning mental distress does not double—it is _____

a. occurrence
b. difference
c. equipped
d. controlling
e. benefited
f. beginning
g. existence
h. equipment
i. equipage
j. transferred
k. reference
l. preferred
m. excellent
n. relaxed
o. picnicking

32. Now test your skill in adding the specified suffixes to these words, applying the doubling rules when appropriate.

a. occur   *ence*   _____

b. differ   *ence*   _____

c. equip   *ed*   _____

d. control   *ing*   _____

e. benefit   *ed*   _____

f. begin   *ing*   _____

g. exist   *ence*   _____

h. equip   *ment*   _____

i. equip   *age*   _____

j. transfer   *ed*   _____

k. refer   *ence*   _____

l. prefer   *ed*   _____

m. excel   *ent*   _____

n. relax   *ed*   _____

o. picnic   *ing*   _____

a. propel
b. control
c. rebel
d. excel
e. compel
f. deter

33. Write the root words from these combined forms.

a. propeller   _____

b. controlled   _____

c. rebellion   _____

d. excelling _____

e. compelled _____

f. deterred _____

POSTTEST

Write the complete words.

1. refer   ence   _____
2. allot   er   _____
3. control   ing   _____
4. gallop   ed   _____
5. prefer   ing   _____
6. excel   ence   _____
7. frolic   some   _____
8. begin   ing   _____
9. confer   ence   _____
10. mimic   ing   _____
11. refer   ed   _____
12. rebel   ion   _____
13. chagrin   ing   _____

14. panic   y   _____
15. visit   or   _____
16. occur   ence   _____
17. skim   ing   _____
18. mimic   ry   _____
19. differ   ence   _____
20. equip   ed   _____
21. relax   ed   _____
22. exist   ence   _____
23. transfer   ing   _____
24. defer   ence   _____
25. conceal   ed   _____

Chapter 11

THE FINAL *E*

When adding a suffix do you drop the final e of a word, or do you keep it? That question is answered in this chapter, and by working carefully through the frames you will learn the rules for dropping or retaining the final e and you will apply the rules to a number of useful words. At the same time you will learn to spell them quickly and unhesitatingly and use them in various contexts. Also you will identify the exceptions to the rules and write them correctly in and out of context.

PRETEST

Add the specified suffixes and write the complete words.

1. desire	*ing*	_____	16. simple	*ly*	_____
2. use	*less*	_____	17. singe	*ing*	_____
3. service	*able*	_____	18. manage	*able*	_____
4. due	*ly*	_____	19. argue	*ing*	_____
5. dense	*ity*	_____	20. adventure	*some*	_____
6. advantage	*ous*	_____	21. dine	*er*	_____
7. come	*ing*	_____	22. canoe	*ist*	_____
8. receive	*able*	_____	23. enforce	*able*	_____
9. argue	*ment*	_____	24. whole	*ly*	_____
10. write	*ing*	_____	25. indispense	*able*	_____
11. true	*ly*	_____	26. nine	*th*	_____
12. change	*able*	_____	27. write	*ing*	_____
13. whole	*some*	_____	28. manage	*ment*	_____
14. advertise	*ment*	_____	29. accurate	*ly*	_____
15. lose	*ing*	_____	30. dye	*ing*	_____

1. When you add a suffix beginning with a *vowel* to a word ending in a silent e you usually drop the e before adding the suffix. Words like *come, write,* or *desire,* end in a silent e—the last sound you hear is the consonant preceding the e: come, write, desire. Words like *thee, devotee,* or *Jeanie,* sound the e so they are not words with the silent e. Notice, too, that the last three end in a double vowel, not a consonant followed by the silent e. Let us look at *come* and the suffix *ing.* Both meet the requirements of the rule so you would drop the e: *coming.*
Check the words below that end in a silent e.

a. use

b. surprise

c. devotee

d. dine

e. relate

f. Swanee

Pick out the suffixes that can require the silent e to be dropped.

a. *ly*
b. *ing*

c. *ment*
d. *able*

e. *some*
f. *ity*

Choose the combinations of words and suffixes to which this rule applies.

a. write   *ing*
b. advise   *ment*
c. desire   *ous*

d. advance   *ed*
e. adventure   *some*
f. vile   *ness*

2. Write the complete words, applying the rule as appropriate.

a. dine   *ing*   _____

b. receive   *able*   _____

c. write   *ing*   _____

d. use   *less*   _____

e. desire   *ous*   _____

f. advertise   *ing*   _____

g. rude   *ness*   _____

3. Now take the word *losing.* It is spelled correctly because
the root word is (*lose, los*) _____
the root ends in a (silent, pronounced) e _____
the suffix begins with a (vowel, consonant) _____
before adding this suffix you (keep, drop) the e_____

Sidebar answers (left column):

a. b. d. e.
b. d. f.
a. c. d.

a. dining
b. receivable
c. writing
d. useless
e. desirous
f. advertising
g. rudeness

lose
silent
vowel
drop

a. desire
b. write
c. conceive
d. suppose
e. hope
f. use

4. The words below have also been formed from roots ending in a silent *e*. So that you will always recognize the parts of such combinations, write the root words.

a. desirous　_____

b. writing　_____

c. conceivable　_____

d. supposed　_____

e. hoping　_____

f. using　_____

a. accuse　accusing
b. receive　received
c. surprise
　　surprising
d. guide　guidance
e. dine　dinette
f. value　valued

5. Now perform two steps: (1) Write the root word from these combinations and then (2) add the specified suffix to it.

	Root	Suffix	Complete word
a. accuser	_____	*ing*	_____
b. receivable	_____	*ed*	_____
c. surprised	_____	*ing*	_____
d. guiding	_____	*ance*	_____
e. dining	_____	*ette*	_____
f. valuable	_____	*ed*	_____

a. writing
b. coming
c. dining
d. pleasurable
e. receivable
f. dividing
g. receiving
h. using
i. density
j. argued
k. indispensable

6. Combine the word and suffixes and write the complete word for each sentence.

a. My cousin is _____ a novel.
　　　　　　　　　　write　*ing*

b. Do you know if Marty is _____?
　　　　　　　　　　　　　come　*ing*

c. When we walked into the cafe we saw Miss Nash
_____ with her niece.
dine　*ing*

d. Sleigh riding is a _____ winter activity.
　　　　　　　　pleasure　*able*

e. Audrey had difficulty understanding the term "_____
　　　　　　　　　　　　　　　　　　　receive　*able*
goods."

f. Uncle Joe is _____ his money between his
　　　　　　　divide　*ing*
daughter and his niece.

g. For several weeks Mr. Green has been _____
mysterious calls.　　　　　　　　　　receive　*ing*

h. How many books are you _____?

                                 use   *ing*

i. We could not see the dome of the Capitol because of the _____ of the fog.

        dense   *ity*

j. Sam and his sister _____ for hours.

                      argue   *ed*

k. Logical thinking is _____ to good writing.

                   indispense   *able*

soft
drop
keep

7. Some "silent e" words with the soft sound of *g* retain the *ge* before certain suffixes, like *able* and *ous*. Take *change,* for instance. The *g* is soft (as in *gem*), not hard (as in *go*). Before suffixes like *ing, er,* or *ed* you follow the rule and drop the e: *changing, changer, changed.* But before the suffix *able* you must keep the e to preserve the soft sound of *g*: *changeable.*
Pronounce the words *manage* and *advantage.*
Do they have the (hard, soft) sound of *g*? _____
Do you (keep, drop) the e before *ing* or *ed*? _____
Do you (keep, drop) the e before *able* or *ous*? _____

a. managing
b. changeable
c. advantageous
d. manageable
e. disadvantaged
f. changer

8. Combine these words and suffixes.

a. manage   *ing*   _____

b. change   *able*   _____

c. advantage   *ous*   _____

d. manage   *able*   _____

e. disadvantage   *ed*   _____

f. change   *er*   _____

soft
drop
keep
• • • • • • • • • • • • •
a. noticing
b. serviceable
c. enforced
d. servicing
e. noticeable
f. enforceable

9. Some "silent e" words with the soft sound of *c* retain the *ce* before the suffix *able.* The *c* in *notice,* for example, has the soft sound (as in *city*) not the hard sound (as in *cat*). For suffixes like *ing, er, ed,* you follow the general rule and drop the e, but for the suffix *able* you keep the e: *noticing—noticeable.*
Now pronounce these: *service enforce*
Do they have the (soft, hard) sound of *c*? _____
Do you (drop, keep) the e before *ing* or *er*? _____
Do you (keep, drop) the e before *able*? _____
• •
Combine the words and suffixes below.

a. notice   *ing*   _____

b. service   *able*   _____

c. enforce *ed* _____

d. service *ing* _____

e. notice *able* _____

f. enforce *able* _____

c. d.

10. Pick out the suffixes that require the e after a soft c or *g* to be kept.

a. *ed* b. *ing* c. *able* d. *ous* f. *er*

a. advantageous
b. noticing
   changeable
c. manageable
   managing
d. enforceable
e. disadvantaged
f. pronounceable

11. Write the complete word for each.

a. The proposal is _____ to both factions.
   advantage ous

b. I kept _____ John's _____
   notice ing   change able

attitude.

c. Although her niece is not _____ Mrs. Brown
   manage able

is _____ to put up with her temper tantrums.
   manage ing

d. That law is not _____.
   enforce able

e. The minority members will be _____ by
   disadvantage ed

the new rules.

f. The words are not _____.
   pronounce able

c. e.
a. b. d. f.

12. You have been adding suffixes beginning with a vowel to words ending in a silent e. Now let us turn to suffixes beginning with a consonant. Generally, the e is retained before such endings. The word *use* is a good example. Before *ing*, *er*, and *ed* you drop the e: *using, user, used.* But before *ful* you keep the e: *useful.* Here is a list of suffixes:

a. *ness* c. *ing* e. *able*
b. *s* d. *ly* f. *ment*

Before which suffixes will you drop the e? _____
Before which will you keep the e? _____

a. using
b. user
c. useless
d. uses
e. useful
f. used
g. usage

13. Now add these suffixes to the root word *use.*

a. *ing* _____ e. *ful* _____

b. *er* _____ f. *ed* _____

c. *less* _____ g. *age* _____

d. *s* _____

a. advertises
b. advertising
c. advertisement
d. advertiser

14. Using *advertise* as the root, add these suffixes to it.

a. *s* _____   c. *ment* _____

b. *ing* _____   d. *er* _____

a. arrangement
b. sincerely
  sincerity
c. accurately
d. ninety

15. Write the complete word(s) for each sentence.

a. What kind of _____ does Sue have for
           arrange   ment
babysitting?

b. Although Tom acts _____ toward his sister,
              sincere   *ly*
his _____ can sometimes be questioned.
       sincere   ity

c. The students computed every example _____.
                          accurate   *ly*

d. In our college over _____ percent of the profes-
              nine   ty
sors are fifty years or older.

ninety
ninth

16. In the preceding frame you simply added *ty* to *nine*
because the *ty* begins with a consonant. Adding *th* to
nine, however, constitutes an exception. So nine + ty =
_____, but nine + th = _____

ninety
ninth

17. Out of a class of one hundred and _____, Henry
                        nine   ty
Bowen was _____ from the top.
       nine   th

drop

18. Another exception is the combination of *argue* and
ment. Even though *ment* begins with a consonant, it is
treated like a suffix beginning with a vowel. So you would
(drop, keep) the e in *argue*. _____

a. argument
b. argued
c. arguing
d. arguable

19. Add these suxffixes to *argue*.

a. *ment* _____   c. *ing* _____

b. *ed* _____   d. *able* _____

arguing
argument

20. Although Tom and Nancy have been _____ for
                          argue   *ing*
an hour, the _____ has not been an emotional
          argue   ment
exchange of words.

REVIEW

a. ninth
b. advertisements
c. coming
d. receiving
e. useful
f. choosing
g. writing
h. scarcity
i. immensity
j. argument
k. ninety
l. useless
m. management

21. Test your skill by writing the complete word(s) for each sentence.

a. Sue was the _____ entry in the beauty contest.
   nine *th*

b. Some _____ can mislead the reader.
   advertise *ments*

c. Are you _____ to the diner soon?
   come *ing*

d. I keep _____ weird phone calls.
   receive *ing*

e. There are several _____ remedies on the market.
   use *ful*

f. What color hat will you be _____?
   choose *ing*

g. An art that is not easy to master is the art of _____.
   write *ing*

h. The heavy rains caused a _____ of berries.
   scarce *ity*

i. The farmer was impressed by the _____ of
   immense *ity*
   the canning factory.

j. Who will lose the _____?
   argue *ment*

k. There were _____ entries.
   nine *ty*

l. To talk any more about the merger is _____.
   use *less*

m. There is friction between employees and _____.
   manage *ment*

a. canoed
b. hoes
c. shoer
d. canoeing
e. hoer
f. shoeing
g. canoeist
h. shoes

22. Words ending in *oe*, like *canoe*, also follow the general rules for keeping the e before a suffix beginning with a consonant or dropping the e before a suffix beginning with a vowel. The one exception is a suffix beginning with *i*—here you must keep the e.
Add the specified suffixes.

a. canoe   *ed*   _____

b. hoe   *s*   _____

c. shoe   *er*   _____

d. canoe   *ing*   _____

e. hoe   er   _____

f. shoe   ing _____

g. canoe   ist _____

h. shoe   s   _____

shoeing

23. Ted is spending his summer _____ his uncle's
                                    shoe ing

horses.

canoed

canoeing

canoeist

24. Although Joan _____ for five hours yesterday,
                       canoe ed

she will go _____ tomorrow because she wants to
             canoe ing

become an expert _____.
                  canoe ist

hoed

25. I've never _____ so much in my life.
                    hoe ed

a. dying
   dyeing

b. singing
   singeing

26. To avoid confusion, the silent e at the end of two
words, *singe* and *dye*, must be retained before *ing*.
Singeing means scorching or burning; *dyeing* means coloring. If you drop the e before the *ing* you will write two
different words: *singing* and *dying*. Choose the appropriate
words for each sentence below.

a. Although Mary's mother was slowly _____
from cancer, she spent an hour yesterday _____
Mary's coat.

b. The cook concentrated so much on her _____
that she didn't do a good job of _____ the hair
from the chicken.

a. dyed

b. singes

c. dyer

d. singeing

e. dyes

f. dyeing

g. singed

27. If the suffix *ing* is the only exception for the words
singe and *dye*, you follow the general rules for either dropping or keeping the final e. Add the specified suffixes to
these two words.

a. dye   ed   _____

b. singe   s   _____

c. dye   er   _____

d. singe   ing _____

e. dye   s   _____

f. dye   ing _____

g. singe   ed   _____

drop
duly
truly
wholly
simply

28. The last four words to be studied *due, true, whole, simple,* follow the general rule for the silent e before a suffix beginning with a consonant except for *ly.*
So before *ly* you would (drop, keep) the e in these four words. _____
Now add *ly* and write the complete words.

_____   _____   _____   _____

a. truly
b. dues
c. simply
d. wholesome
e. trues
f. duly
g. trueness
h. wholly
i. wholeness

29. Write the complete words for all these "silent e" words.

a. true   *ly*   _____

b. due   *s*   _____

c. simple   *ly*   _____

d. whole   *some*   _____

e. true   *s*   _____

f. due   *ly*   _____

g. true   *ness*   _____

h. whole   *ly*   _____

i. whole   *ness*   _____

due
true
whole
simple

30. Name the four words that drop the final e before *ly.*

_____   _____   _____   _____

REVIEW

a. wholly
b. hoeing
  canoeing
c. dyeing
d. truly
e. singeing
f. shoed
g. duly
h. wholesome

31. Add the words and suffixes and write the complete words.

a. His actions were _____ unforgivable.
                        whole ly

b. While the boys spent the afternoon _____, the
                                        hoe   ing
girls went _____.
            canoe ing

c. The process of putting coloring permanently into fibers of cotton or wool is called _____.
                        dye ing

d. I am _____ sorry for my rudeness.
        true ly

e. Susan keeps _____ her hair with the hot
                    singe   ing
curling iron.

f. The blacksmith _____ all the horses yesterday.
   shoe ed

g. The newly elected commissioner will begin his reform program within a _____ specified time.
   due ly

h. Her two nephews are _____ youngsters.
   whole some

POSTTEST

Add the specified suffix to each word and write the complete word.

1. achieve	ment	_____	16. simple	ly	_____
2. advise	able	_____	17. receive	ing	_____
3. canoe	ing	_____	18. dense	ity	_____
4. pleasure	able	_____	19. pursue	er	_____
5. manage	able	_____	20. whole	ly	_____
6. age	less	_____	21. change	able	_____
7. canoe	ist	_____	22. ache	ing	_____
8. notice	able	_____	23. desire	ous	_____
9. judge	ing	_____	24. advantage	ous	_____
10. remote	ness	_____	25. rare	ity	_____
11. true	ly	_____	26. achieve	ing	_____
12. true	ness	_____	27. imagine	able	_____
13. singe	ing	_____	28. hoe	ing	_____
14. disadvantage	ed	_____	29. argue	ment	_____
15. argue	ing	_____	30. pronounce	able	_____

Chapter 12

THE FINAL Y

Have you had words like *studying, angrily,* or *tries* under-scored and marked with "sp" in the margin? Even if this has only happened occasionally, this chapter will be worthwhile for you to read, because by the end of it you will know when to keep the *y* or when to change it to *i* before a suffix. By learning and applying the rules and spelling a number of common and useful "final y" words, both in and out of context, you will master the techniques needed to distinguish between those words that follow the rules and those that do not, and to recognize the excep-tions immediately. In the case of plurals of words ending in y, you will spell them accurately as well as reduce them to their singular form, ensuring the spelling of both forms correctly at all times.

PRETEST

Combine the root and suffix and write the complete word.

1. accompany	*ment*	_____	11. apply	*ing*	_____
2. convey	*s*	_____	12. happy	*ly*	_____
3. occupy	*ing*	_____	13. carry	*ing*	_____
4. copy	*ist*	_____	14. hungry	*ly*	_____
5. story	*es*	_____	15. beauty	*ful*	_____
6. bury	*al*	_____	16. dormitory	*es*	_____
7. beauty	*es*	_____	17. happy	*ness*	_____
8. employ	*er*	_____	18. day	*ly*	_____
9. try	*es*	_____	19. study	*ing*	_____
10. tragedy	*es*	_____	20. pity	*ful*	_____

21. display   *ing*   _____
22. company   es   _____
23. pity   *ing*   _____
24. cozy   *ly*   _____
25. chimney   s   _____

26. society   es   _____
27. try   *al*   _____
28. theory   es   _____
29. accompany   ed   _____
30. industry   es   _____

a. d. e.
. . . .
b. relaying
c. surveys
e. displayed
g. destroyer
h. alleys

1. Here is the general rule: when a final *y* is preceded by a *vowel*, you keep the *y* before adding a suffix. Take *journey*, which ends in *y* preceded by the vowel *e*. If you add *s* to form the plural, or *ed* or *ing* to make verb forms, you keep the *y*: *journeys, journeyed, journeying*. How about the noun *penny?* or *party?* Both end in *y* but both are preceded by a consonant. So these words do not meet the requirements of the rule.

From the list below identify those words to which this final *y* rule applies.

a. relay   _____   d. destroy   _____

b. pity   _____   e. monkey   _____

c. hungry   _____   f. clumsy   _____
. . . .
Now pick out only those words to which the rule applies, add the specified suffixes, and write the complete words.

a. beauty   *es*   _____

b. relay   *ing*   _____

c. survey   *s*   _____

d. baby   *es*   _____

e. display   *ed*   _____

f. duty   *es*   _____

g. destroy   *er*   _____

h. alley   *s*   _____

a. medleys
b. trolleys
c. pulleys
d. destroyed
e. portrayal
f. surveying
g. chimneys

2. Write the complete word for each sentence.

a. The symphony played several _____ in last
night's concert.   medley s

b. Electric cars can also be called _____.
                                      trolley s

c. The heavy concrete blocks were lifted to the top of the tower by _____.
                              pulley s

d. During the air raids in England, many buildings were

_____.
     destroy *ed*

e. I was amused by his _____ of the school-

           portray *al*

teacher.

f. Mike Jones earns his living by _____ the land

         survey *ing*

for highway construction.

g. Black smoke billowed from the two _____.

         chimney *s*

vowel

keep

3. The rule illustrated by the words and suffixes you added above can be stated as: When adding a suffix to a word ending in final *y* preceded by a (vowel, consonant), you (keep, drop) the *y* and add the suffix.

REVIEW

a. enjoyable
b. employment
d. conveyed
e. delaying
g. buyers

4. Combine the words and suffixes below to which this final *y* rule applies. Leave blank any combination that does not follow the rule.

a. Her trip to Peru was _____.

       enjoy *able*

b. I will look for different _____.

       employ *ment*

c. Researchers have found a new feeding formula for

_____.
    baby *es*

d. Her message to the board was _____ yesterday.

       convey *ed*

e. There is no use _____ any longer.

     delay *ing*

f. His information was not _____.

      rely *able*

g. How many fashion _____ does the store have?

     buy *ers*

5. Whereas the final *y* preceded by a vowel is usually re-tained before a suffix, the final *y* preceded by a consonant is changed to *i* before suffixes that do *not* begin with *i*. For those that begin with *i* you keep the *y*. For example, to form the plural of *copy*, you change the *y* to *i* and add *es*:

a. c. d. f. g.
• • • • • • • • • • • • •
a. c. d. e.
• • • • • • • • • • • • •
i
• • • • • • • • • • • • •
a. b. d. f.

copies. Using *copy* as the root word, let us add these suffixes:

copy + *er* = copier
copy + *ed* = copied   but   copy + *ist* = copyist
copy + *ing* = copying

Check the words below that have the final *y* preceded by a consonant:

a. cemetery _____   e. survey   _____
b. pulley   _____   f. tragedy   _____
c. story   _____   g. dictionary _____
d. county   _____

• •

Check before which suffixes listed below the final *y* preceded by a consonant is changed to *i*.

a. *er*   _____   d. *ness* _____
b. *ing* _____   e. *s*   _____
c. *ly*   _____   f. *ist*   _____

• •

The suffixes that require the final *y* preceded by a consonant to keep the *y* begin with what letter? _____

• •

From the list below identify which combinations require the *y* to be changed to *i*.

a. mercy *ful* _____   e. study *ing* _____
b. steady *ly*   _____   f. pity   *es*   _____
c. copy   *ing* _____   g. lobby *ist* _____
d. bury   *al*   _____

a. varying
b. accompanies
c. enemies
d. reliance
e. pitying
f. cemeteries
g. angrily
h. societies
i. wealthier
j. clumsily
k. pennies
l. studying

6. Now add the suffixes to these "final *y*" words.

a. vary   *ing*   _____

b. accompany *es*   _____

c. enemy   *es*   _____

d. rely   *ance* _____

e. pity   *ing*   _____

f. cemetery *es*   _____

g. angry   *ly*   _____

h. society   *es*   _____

i. wealthy   *er*   _____

j. clumsy   *ly*   _____

k. penny   *es*   _____

l. study   *ing*   _____

a. denied
b. occupying
c. beautiful
d. relies
e. carrying
f. heartily
g. studying

7. Now write the complete words for these sentences.

a. The captured enemy tried to establish his innocence when he _____ any responsibility for the raid.
deny   ed

b. This summer the study of plane geometry is _____
occupy   ing
most of Andy's time.

c. The reigning queen is _____.
beauty   ful

d. The manger _____ too much on his employees.
rely   es

e. Yesterday John carried two heavy trunks to the attic, but today he is _____ small cartons up there.
carry   ing

f. After a good night's sleep, Mary ate _____.
hearty   ly

g. Nora has been _____ too hard.
study   ing

days
daily

8. The rule for final *y* preceded by a vowel applies to the word *day*, except for the suffix *ly*.
Combine *day* and the plural suffix *s*. _____
Now combine *day* and *ly*. _____

a. said
b. laid

9. Like *day*, the words *lay* and *say* generally follow the rule. When you add the past tense ending *ed*, however, you must change the *y* to *i* and drop the *e* in *ed*.
Complete these sentences:

a. I say something today, but I _____ it yesterday.

b. Today I lay the book on the chest; yesterday I _____ it there.

b.

10. For the past tense ending *ed*, the word *pay* is treated like *lay* and *say*. But there are two meanings to *pay*. If it means to coat or cover (a ship, for example) with tar or asphalt, you have a choice of spelling: *paid* or *payed*. If *pay* means to compensate, to give money in exchange, then you always write *paid*.
Which sentence below does not allow for an alternate spelling:

a. Twenty workmen _____ the seams of the U.S.S. Harrington in five days.

b. John _____ a hundred dollars for his recorder.

paid or payed

a. saying
b. payed or paid
c. layer
d. said
e. days
f. paid
g. laid

a. laid
b. said
c. daily
d. payed or paid
e. laying
f. payable
g. payer paid
payee

11. What are the spellings allowed for sentence a. in the preceding frame? _____

12. Now add the suffixes to these.

a. say *ing* _____   e. day *s* _____

b. pay *ed* _____   f. pay *ed* _____
   (to coat)   (to recompense)

c. lay *er* _____   g. lay *ed* _____

d. say *ed* _____

13. Combine these words and suffixes.

a. The grandmother _____ the child in her crib.
                       lay ed

b. How many times have you _____ it?
                       say ed

c. The railroad has a _____ run to Kensington.
                       day ly

d. The men stopped working for the day when they _____ the seams.
         pay ed

e. John is _____ new tile.
                lay ing

f. The loan is _____ on the first of each month.
                pay able

g. The person who pays the money is the _____ ;
                             pay er
   the person to whom the money is _____ is the _____ .
                       pay ed   *pay ee*

day
society

14. To avoid misspelling some root words, let us reverse the procedure of adding elements. With suffixes being added to a word ending in final *y* preceded by a vowel you simply add the suffix, so in subtracting the suffix you just take it off: *toys* − *s* = *toy*. For a word ending in *y* preceded by a consonant you change the *y* to *i* and add the suffix, so in subtracting the suffix you take off the suffix and replace the *i* with the *y*: *relies* − *es* − *i* + *y* = *rely*. What is the singular form of *days*? _____
What is the singular form of *societies*? _____

company

15. The word *companies* means several establishments. Just one establishment would be a _____.

lobbies
lobby

16. The hotel has several _____. Just one
                            lobby es
would be a _____.

REVIEW

a. denial
b. pities
c. lobbying
d. steadier
e. tragedies
f. cozily
g. cemeteries
h. copyist
i. tries
j. accompanied

17. Test your skill by writing the complete word for each blank.

a. deny   al   _____   f.   cozy   ly   _____

b. pity   es   _____   g.   cemetery   es   _____

c. lobby   ing   _____   h.   copy   ist   _____

d. steady   er   _____   i.   try   es   _____

e. tragedy   es   _____   j.   accompany   ed   _____

change the y to i
keep

18. Let us restate this rule for the final *y* preceded by a consonant: before adding a suffix that does not begin with *i*, you (keep the *y*, change the *y* to *i*). _____
Before a suffix like *ist*, you (drop, keep) the *y*. _____

kept

19. Generally, the final *y* preceded by a vowel is (kept, dropped) before the suffix. _____

a. denial   denies
   denied   denying
b. portrayal
   portraying
   portrayed
   portrays

20. Now apply the rules to these.

a. deny   b. portray

        al   _____   al   _____

        es   _____   ing   _____

        ed   _____   ed   _____

        ing   _____   s   _____

paid

21. How do you spell the past tense of *pay*, meaning to exchange money? _____

POSTTEST

Combine the roots and suffixes and write the complete words.

1. summary   es   _____   9.   pay   ed   _____
                                          (to recompense)

2. annoy   ance   _____   10.   monkey   s   _____

3. copy   er   _____   11.   society   es   _____

4. rely   es   _____   12.   employ   ed   _____

5. portray   s   _____   13.   lobby   ing   _____

6. defy   ing   _____   14.   medley   s   _____

7. bury   al   _____   15.   cemetery   es   _____

8. day   ly   _____

16. tendency   es   _____
17. accompany   ment   _____
18. key   ed   _____
19. try   ing   _____
20. lay   ed   _____
21. copy   ist   _____
22. university   es   _____
23. controversy   es   _____

24. pity   less   _____
25. ready   ing   _____
26. deny   al   _____
27. luxury   es   _____
28. employ   ment   _____
29. say   ed   _____
30. academy   es   _____

Chapter 13

IE OR EI

If you have been plagued by the *ie* and *ei* combinations, wondering when to use one or the other, you need not worry any longer. This chapter will present definite rules for the *ie* and *ei* combinations as well as some exceptions to these rules. In the chapter you will (1) identify the various vowel sounds represented by *ie* or *ei*; (2) apply the rules for combining the e and i; (3) recognize and spell correctly the exceptions; and (4) practice spelling a number of useful "ei-ie" words in and out of context. The chapter will also give you a basis for spelling other familiar or unfamiliar "i" and "e" words.

PRETEST

Fill in the correct combination: *ie* or *ei*.

1. To ease means to rel____ve.
2. Vanity is another name for conc____t.
3. To get is to rec____ve.
4. Two young boys were credited with the s____zure of the bank robber.
5. To be lacking in something is to be defic____nt.
6. The postman w____ghed my packages.
7. The head of a tribe is usually called a ch____f.
8. Please give me a p____ce of cake.
9. Strange is a synonym for w____rd.
10. Another word for forgery is counterf____t.
11. What is your h____ght and w____ght?
12. To accomplish means to ach____ve.
13. I expect to join the for____gn service.
14. We live in a blighted n____ghborhood.
15. How much l____sure time do you want?

Yes
· · · · · · · · · · · · · ·
d.

1. One of the best ways to select the correct combinations of *i* and *e* is by their sound, as the vowel sound represented by these two letters will usually provide the clue to the correct spelling of a word.

Look at these words carefully, then say them aloud, stressing the underlined part.

piece	niece	siege
chief	deceive	relief
receive	yield	conceit

Check whether the vowel sound of the *i* and *e* is the same for all the words.

Yes _____ No _____

· ·

The vowel sound matches which sound in the underlined portions of the words below? _____

a. bed   b. bay   c. bite   d. beef

no yes

2. The vowel sound in *beef* is the same as the speech sound represented by the letter *e*—this we call the long *e* sound. Each word in the list you just pronounced has this long *e* sound. But the spelling of the *i* and *e* is not the same. Look again at the words:

piece	receive
chief	deceive
niece	conceit
siege	
relief	

The first list has the *ie* and the second *ei*. In the first is the consonant preceding *ie* always the same? _____ Is it in the second? _____ .

ie
ei

3. The consonant then provides the clue. If the consonant is *not* c, you write which combination (*ie, ei*)? _____
If the consonant is *c*, you write it like this: _____ .

a. *ie*
b. *ei*
c. *ie*
d. *ie*
e. *ei*
f. *ie*
g. *ei*

4. Each word below has the long *e* sound. Write in the correct combination: *ie* or *ei*.

a. y____ld   e. conc____t

b. rec____pt   f. bel____ved

c. s____ge   g. rec____ving

d. ch____f

a. *ei*
b. *ie*
c. *ie*
d. *ie*
e. *ei*
f. *ie*
g. *ei*

5. Complete the words in these sentences with *ie* or *ei*.

a. She has no cause to dec_____ve.

b. Betsy has only one n_____ce.

c. The army ended its long s_____ge.

d. His statement is hard for me to bel_____ve.

e. My aunt has many cash rec_____pts.

f. Please give me a p_____ce of paper.

g. Lou is more conc_____ted than Ted.

a. receive
b. siege
c. achieve
d. relieve
e. deceive

6. At the left is a panel of words requiring *ie* or *ei*. Read each sentence carefully for its meaning, choose the word from the panel, and write the complete word.

dec_____ve   a. The principal said I would _____
s_____ge   a prize.
ach_____ve   b. The fortress withstood the _____
rec_____ve   for a full month.
rel_____ve   c. I worry that I may not _____
              accomplish
              my goal.
              d. Many new drugs help to _____
              discomfort.
              e. A person who will mislead another will
              _____ him.

ie   ei

7. The usual spelling of *i* and *e* with the long *e* sound is _____ except after *c*; then it is _____.

yes
receive
c

8. Now let us take these words. Look at them closely and pronounce them.

weird   seize   either
leisure   seizure   neither

Do they have the same sound as bel*ie*f and receive? _____
Is the combination of *i* and *e* written as in *belief* or *receive*? _____
To best remember them you can link them with those words with the long *e* sound coming after which consonant? _____

neither
seizure
leisure
weird

9. You can also associate them in some way. For example, two have similar sounds: *either* and n_____.
Another two go together: the verb *seize* and its noun s_____ure. Another rhymes with seizure: l_____.
The one that stands alone is w_____rd, meaning strange.

a. either
b. neither
c. seize
d. seizure
e. leisure
f. weird

10. Finish spelling the exceptions:

a. One or another is the definition of e_____.

b. Not one or the other is the meaning of *n*_____.

c. To grasp is to s_____.

d. The act of grasping is s_____.

e. Free time is called l_____.

f. To be strange is to be w_____.

either
neither
seize
seizure
leisure
weird

11. Write the six exceptions to the long e sound of *i* and *e*.

_____ _____ _____ _____ _____ _____

no

REVIEW

12. Look at this group of words. Are there any *i*'s and *e*'s out of order? _____

conceive	conceit	receipt
achieve	receive	thief
relief	believe	belief

a. *ie*
b. *ei*
c. *ei*
d. *ei*
e. *ei*
f. *ei*
g. *ie*
h. *ei*

13. Supply the missing *ie* or *ei*.

a. Do you bel_____ve his story?

b. N_____ther Ann nor I will go.

c. Strange is the meaning of *w*_____*rd*.

d. How much money will he rec_____ve?

e. Mary Jo has too much l_____sure.

f. The three men tried to s_____ze her.

g. I hope to ach_____ve my goals.

h. Joe is terribly conc_____ted.

c.

14. Check which sound in the underlined portion of the following words matches the sound of the *i* and *e* in the words to the right.

a. b<u>i</u>t   neighbor

b. b<u>ee</u>f   freight

c. b<u>ay</u>   weigh

d. b<u>i</u>te

c. e. f. h.

15. All the words below have the *ei* combination. Pick out those with the long *a* sound as in bay.

a. either   e. reign
b. weird   f. reindeer
c. weighty   g. seize
d. leisure   h. sleigh

ei

16. Like the six exceptions to the long e sound, the words with the long *a* sound have which combination (*ie, ei*)?

_____

yes—all are
spelled *ei*

17. Does the long *a* rule apply to the underlined words?

_____

a. During the Reign of Terror thousands of people were executed.
b. Joe hopped on a freight car.
c. One controls a horse with reins.
d. My mother is overweight.
e. Reindeer Lake is in Manitoba.

a. long *a*
b. long *e*
c. long *e*
d. long *a*
e. long *e*
f. long *e*
g. long *a*

18. Now indicate which sound each *i* and *e* combination has.

a. weight   _____   e. leisure   _____

b. weird   _____   f. neither   _____

c. seizure   _____   g. neighbor   _____

d. freight   _____

b.

19. In the preceding frame, the words having the long e sound
a. followed the rule for long e.
b. were exceptions to this rule.

a. *ei*
b. *ei*
c. *ei*
d. *ei*

20. Read the sentences first, then fill in the missing *i* and e combinations.

a. Women like v____ls on their hats.

b. A pleasurable sport in the winter is a sl____gh ride.

c. A vessel that carries blood back to the heart is a v____n.

d. How much do you w____gh?

ie
ei
ei

21. Generally, the long e sound of *i* and *e* is written _____ except after c when it is written _____; the long sound of a is written _____.

b.

22. Now pronounce the word *height*. The *ei* corresponds to which sound? _____

a. b<u>e</u>d   b. b<u>i</u>te   c. b<u>ee</u>f   d. b<u>i</u>t

e. b<u>ay</u>

ei

23. Both the long *a* and long *i* sounds are written (*ie* or *ei*)? _____

ei

24. When one measures how tall he is, he measures his h_____ght.

height

25. The word meaning tallness is often misspelled not only because of the *ei*, but because of the ending: Johnny is nearly the h_____gh_____ of his father.

a. ei ei
b. ei
c. ei
d. ei
e. ei

26. Read each sentence first, then write the correct combination(s) of *i* and *e*.

a. What is your w_____ght and h_____ght?

b. The troops numbered _____ghty thousand.

c. I wonder how long this king will r_____gn.

d. After dark Tim sneaked down to hop on a fr_____ght.

e. If you want to control your horse, tighten the r_____ns.

d.

27. Now look at these words closely and pronounce them:
        foreign   counterfeit
The sound of the *ei* corresponds to which underlined sound below:

a. b<u>ay</u>   b. b<u>i</u>te   c. b<u>ee</u>f   d. b<u>i</u>t

ei ei

28. The short *i* sound is in the words *counterf_____t* and *for_____gn*.

feit

29. An imitation or forgery is the definition of the noun *counter_____*.

eign

30. To be alien to one's nature is to be for_____ to it.

ei
ei ei

31. The short *i* is also apparent in three other words: *forf_____t   surf_____t   sover_____gn*

feit
feit

32. To surrender a privilege for committing an offense is to for_____; to feed to excess or to overindulge is to sur_____.

ei

33. A king or queen can also be called a sover_____gn.

counterfeit
surfeit
forfeit

34. Three words having the same short *i* sound of *i* and *e* are _____*feit*, _____*feit*, and _____ *feit*.

foreign
sovereign

35. Two words having the same ending with the short *i* sound of *i* and *e* are _____*gn* and _____*gn*.

REVIEW

a. *ei*   short *i*
b. *ei*   long *a*
c. *ei*   long *i*
d. *ei*   short *i*
e. *ei*   long *a*
f. *ei*   short *i*
g. *ei*   long *a*

36. Fill in the missing *i* and *e* combinations for each word and identify the vowel sound of each.

Vowel
sound

Vowel
sound

a. for_____gn   _____
b. w_____ghty   _____
c. h_____ght   _____
d. counterf_____t   _____

e. r_____gn   _____
f. forf_____t   _____
g. r_____ndeer   _____

long *a*
long *i*
short *i*

37. The *ei* combination has three vowel sounds: _____ *a*, _____ *i*, and _____ *i*.

a. *eign*
b. *eigh*   *ei*
c. *feit*
a. *eight*
e. *feit*
f. *eigners*

38. Now complete the "ie-ei" words.

a. Nancy accepted a job in the for_____ service.

b. Only five boys w_____ over _____ghty pounds.

c. John must for_____ a day's pay.

d. Roger's h_____ prevents him from playing basketball.

e. Sam was convicted of printing counter_____ money.

f. The U.S. admits a quota of for_____ each year.

shent

39. Now let us take *efficient* and divide it first into syllables: ef   fi   cient. Pronounce them. The last has which sound ("sent," "shent")? _____

the "sh"

40. Since we are interested in the *i* and *e*, what part of the "shent" sound in *cient* does the *cie* have?

cie

41. This "sh" sound then is represented by the letters _____.

yes

42. Do these adjectives also have the "sh" sound of *cie*?

_____

proficient   sufficient   deficient

second and third
(*fi   cient*)

43. Let us look at the four words again: *proficient, sufficient, deficient, efficient.* Which two syllables are spelled the same? _____

ef suf
pro
de

44. Only the first syllable differs. To be effective is to be _____ficient; to be enough, or to suffice, is to be _____ficient. The prefix *pro* means forward and *de* means away or down. If one is skilled in a trade (gone forward, in other words) he is said to be _____ficient; if he has gone down or is lacking in some way he is _____ficient.

a. sufficient
b. efficient
c. deficient
d. proficient

45. Write the correct "shent" words for each sentence.

a. There will be _____ food for the
                                   enough
picnic.

b. This is the most _____ way to
                              effective
operate the machine.

c. In spite of his education, he is _____
                                          wanting
in his knowledge of the English language.

d. In his layout work at the printshop he is _____.
                                                    skilled

t
cy

46. The state of being efficient is *efficiency.* In spelling the noun you drop the ____ from the adjective and add

____.

a. sufficiency
b. deficiency
c. proficiency

47. How would you spell these nouns?

a. the state of being enough _____

b. the state of being wanting _____

c. the state of being skilled _____

REVIEW

cie

48. When *i* and *e* are preceded by *c* and have the "sh" sound, the letters are combined like this: _____.

a. deficient
b. sufficient
c. efficient
d. proficient
e. efficiency

49. Supply the "cie" words to fit each definition.

a. to be wanting _____

b. to be enough _____

c. to be effective _____

d. to be skilled _____

e. the state of being
effective _____

POSTTEST

Fill in the correct combination: *ie* or *ei*.

1. I cannot bel____ve your story.

2. The Army finally ended its long s____ge.

3. He thinks he has a sover____gn right to do that.

4. Where is the fr____ght office?

6. He must forf____t all his privileges.

7. Have you seen any r____ndeer?

8. Mr. Black is very effic____nt.

9. Don't y____ld to his demands.

10. As he comes around the corner, try to s____ze him.

11. How much do you w____gh?

12. To be lacking means to be defic____nt.

13. He has a reputation as a th____f.

14. I am working so hard I have no l____sure time.

15. The girl told a w____rd story.

Chapter 14

PLURALS

There are just two plural endings, but not knowing when to use one or the other can present some problems. In this chapter you will learn specific rules for each ending, apply the rules to a number of words and write these plurals in context, recognize the exceptions and spell them correctly. You will also change various plurals back to the singular so that you will not misspell either form.

PRETEST

Write the plurals of the following nouns.

1. display   _____
2. penalty   _____
3. gas   _____
4. veto   _____
5. zoo   _____
6. monarch   _____
7. inquiry   _____
8. crisis   _____
9. Negro   _____
10. melody   _____
11. perch   _____
12. thief   _____
13. potato   _____
14. Tommy   _____
15. wish   _____

16. buzz   _____
17. university   _____
18. Tory   _____
19. discrepancy   _____
20. grief   _____
21. half   _____
22. society   _____
23. gulf   _____
24. elegy   _____
25. datum   _____
26. hero   _____
27. wife   _____
28. study   _____
29. decoy   _____
30. tax   _____

a. princesses
b. airships
c. clutches
d. seedlings
e. crashes
f. concerts
g. wishes
h. screens
i. pitches
j. addresses
k. matches

1. Two suffixes are used to form the plural from the singular: *s* and *es*. Most words take just *s*. For instance, the plural of *table* is *tables*, of *book* is *books*, and of *chair* is *chairs*. Certain other words need *es* to form the plural because just an *s* would make them difficult or impossible to pronounce. Take *dress* or *gas* that already end in *s*. Another *s* would only extend the original "s" sound, not make another syllable that is needed to pronounce the plural: *dress es, gas es*. The same problem applies to words ending in *sh* and *tch*. If you try pronouncing *dish* and *ditch* with just another *s* (as in *dishs* and *ditchs*) you will hear just an "s" sound after the *sh* or *tch*, not a distinct syllable, as in *dish es* or *ditch es*.

Apply these rules to make the plural forms of the nouns below.

a. princess _____   g. wish _____

b. airship _____   h. screen _____

c. clutch _____   i. pitch _____

d. seedling _____   j. address _____

e. crash _____   k. match _____

f. concert _____

taxes   buzzes

2. Like those words ending in *s*, *sh*, and *tch*, those ending in *x* and *z*, like *tax* and *buzz*, need more than the *s* to form a pronounceable plural ending. How would you write the plurals of tax and buzz? _____ _____

a. S   d. S
b. S   e. H
c. H   f. S
• • • • • • • • • • • • • •
arches   lurches
monarchs   peaches
epochs   porches

3. The plural ending for a word ending in *ch* depends on the sound of the *ch*. If it has the soft sound (as in *church*) you add *es*. If it has the hard sound (as in *epoch*) you add *s*.

Indicate by S (soft) or H (hard) which sound of *ch* these words have.

a. arch _____   d. peach _____

b. lurch _____   e. epoch _____

c. monarch _____   f. porch _____
• •
Now add the correct plural endings to the above words.

_____   _____   _____

_____   _____   _____

s sh ch (soft sound)
tch x z

4. Now we have another general rule for forming plurals. Using this list as a guide, write the consonant endings that require *es*: _____

dress   bush   porch   match   fox   waltz

es

5. Words ending in s, *sh, ch* (soft), *x*, and *z* take _____ to form the plural.

a. matches
b. transplants
c. bungalows
d. dishes
e. monarchs
f. organs
g. taxes
h. splashes
i. stairs
j. compresses
k. bookcases
l. pitches
m. waltzes
n. lurches

6. Apply the rules presented thus far and form the plurals.

a. match _____   h. splash _____

b. transplant _____   i. stair _____

c. bungalow _____   j. compress _____

d. dish _____   k. bookcase _____

e. monarch _____   l. pitch _____

f. organ _____   m. waltz _____

g. tax _____   n. lurch _____

a. s
b. es
c. s
d. es
e. es
f. s
g. s
h. es
i. es
j. s
k. es
l. s

7. Nouns ending in y preceded by a vowel usually take s to form the plural. For example, *attorney* ends in y preceded by e, so its plural is *attorneys*. On the other hand, most nouns ending in y preceded by a consonant take es and the y is changed to i before the es. *Party* ends in y preceded by t, so its plural is *parties*.
From the list below decide which words take s and which take es.

a. decoy _____   g. pulley _____

b. lullaby _____   h. dormitory _____

c. tray _____   i. tragedy _____

d. clergy _____   j. display _____

e. melody _____   k. duty _____

f. bay _____   l. attorney _____

a. studies
b. ploys
c. days
d. elegies
e. dailies
f. replies
g. buoys
h. inquiries
i. frays
j. cemeteries
k. trolleys
l. joys

8. Now write the plurals for these singular nouns.

a. study _____   g. buoy _____

b. ploy _____   h. inquiry _____

c. day _____   i. fray _____

d. elegy _____   j. cemetery _____

e. daily _____   k. trolley _____

f. reply _____   l. joy _____

a. Bettys   Tonys
b. Kellys

9. Proper names (first and last) ending in *y* preceded by either a vowel or consonant take *s* so that the name will not be changed. For instance, the Kennedy family can be called the Kennedys. More than one Libby would be Libbys and more than one boy named Harry would be Harrys. Some proper nouns, however, take *es* because they are not names of specific individuals. The plural of *Tory* (a member of a British political party in the seventeenth century) would be *Tories*. Note that the *y* is changed to *i* before adding *es*.

a. If you write about several girls named Betty and several boys named Tony, how would you write the plurals?

_____   _____

b. All the members of the Kelly family would be called the _____.

a. deputies
b. Anthonys
c. properties
d. Crosbys
e. Tories
f. societies

10. Write the correct plurals for these words.

a. deputy   _____   d. Crosby   _____

b. Anthony _____   e. Tory   _____

c. property _____   f. society _____

a. drays
b. Sibleys
c. countries
d. envoys
e. Henrys
f. plays
g. treaties
h. counties

11. Now apply all the rules about plurals you have learned thus far and write the correct forms for these words ending in *y*.

a. dray   _____   e. Henry   _____

b. Sibley _____   f. play   _____

c. country _____   g. treaty _____

d. envoy   _____   h. county _____

a. d. e. f.
b. c.

12. Sometimes the singular form is incorrectly formed from the plural. So that you do not make this mistake, let us practice forming the singular. As you remember, you form the plural of words ending in *y* preceded by a vowel by adding *s*. The singular is formed by subtracting the *s*. For words ending in *y* preceded by a consonant you must subtract *es* and change the *i* back to the original *y*.
Which of the following would end in *y* preceded by a consonant in the singular? _____

a. discrepancies   d. bullies

b. holidays   e. cemeteries

c. chimneys   f. lobbies

To form the singular which ones would have the *s* subtracted? _____

a. discrepancy
b. bully
c. cemetery
d. lobby

a. societies
d. lobby
f. tries
g. tragedy

13. Write the singular forms for each word below.

a. discrepancies _____   c. cemeteries _____

b. bullies _____   d. lobbies _____

14. The endings of some words below are misspelled. By applying the rules, identify the incorrect words and spell them correctly.

a. societys _____   e. chimneys _____

b. surveys _____   f. trys _____

c. studies _____   g. tragedie _____

d. lobbie _____

REVIEW

a. valleys
b. Woodburys
tragedies
c. addresses
d. taxes
e. waltzes
f. Februarys
g. columns
h. comedies
i. ditches

15. Now test your skill by writing the plural noun(s) for each sentence.

a. The ranches were built only in the _____.
valley

b. The _____ have suffered many
Woodbury

_____.
tragedy

c. How many _____ does he have?
address

d. The legislature is trying to reduce _____.
tax

e. For the next orchestra concert the conductor has selected two _____.
waltz

f. Minnesota _____ are cold.
February

g. The auditorium has six Doric _____.
column

h. The last two Broadway hits are both _____.
comedy

i. The farmers are busy digging irrigation _____.
ditch

es

16. Which plural ending do you use with words ending in s, sh, ch (soft), tch, s, and z? _____

cries

17. How do you form the plural of cry? _____

displays

18. Write the plural of *display*. _____

---

a. zoos
b. tomatoes
c. photos
d. radios
e. echoes
f. potatoes
g. Negroes
h. boos
i. vetoes
j. silos
k. heroes
l. torpedoes

19. Most nouns ending in o preceded by either a vowel or a consonant take s. Seven words, however, are exceptions: *echo, hero, Negro, potato, tomato, torpedo,* and *veto.*
Write the plurals of these "o" words.

a. zoo _____   g. Negro _____

b. tomato _____   h. boo _____

c. photo _____   i. veto _____

d. radio _____   j. silo _____

e. echo _____   k. hero _____

f. potato _____   l. torpedo _____

---

a. Negroes
b. heroes   potatoes
tomatoes
c. Echoes   vetoes
d. torpedoes

20. Perhaps an easy way to remember the exceptions is to place them in a context. Read the sentences below and supply the plural forms.

a. Some blacks prefer to be called _____.
                                                   Negro

b. The _____ like _____ and
          hero   potato

_____.
      tomato

c. _____ of the speeches condemning the gov-
      Echo
ernor's _____ rang through the corridors.
      veto

d. The twenty-year-old sailor fired the decisive _____.
                                            torpedo

---

a. silos
b. sopranos
c. potatoes
d. torpedoes
e. pianos
f. vetoes
g. bassos
h. ratios
i. Negroes
j. altos
k. rodeos
l. heroes
m. zoos
n. echoes

21. Now test your skill in writing the plurals for these words.

a. silo _____   h. ratio _____

b. soprano _____   i. Negro _____

c. potato _____   j. alto _____

d. torpedo _____   k. rodeo _____

e. piano _____   l. hero _____

f. veto _____   m. zoo _____

g. basso _____   n. echo _____

Negro
hero
potato
tomato
echo
veto
torpedo

a. rodeo
b. tomato
c. piano
d. veto
e. Negro
f. kangaroo
g. torpedo
h. ratio
i. hero
j. potato

22. Name the seven words ending in o that do not take s to form the plural.

_____   _____
_____   _____
_____   _____
_____

23. Since it is important to spell the singular as well as the plural correctly, let us reverse the procedure and write the singular from the plural. For example, to reduce zoos you simply take off the s: zoo. Echoes has the es ending, so the singular would be echo. Now reduce these plurals to their singular forms.

a. rodeos   _____   f. kangaroos   _____

b. tomatoes _____   g. torpedoes   _____

c. pianos   _____   h. ratios   _____

d. vetoes   _____   i. heroes   _____

e. Negroes   _____   j. potatoes   _____

a. griefs
b. sheriffs
c. fifes

24. To form the plural of nouns ending in f, fe, or ff, you usually add s. For instance, the plural of belief is beliefs, of strife is strifes, and of tariff is tariffs. What would be the plurals for these?

a. grief   _____   c. fife   _____

b. sheriff _____

a. elves
b. shelves
c. halves
d. leaves
e. thieves
f. wolves

25. Certain words ending in f or fe change their ending to ves to form the plural. Write the plurals of these words:

a. elf   _____   d. leaf   _____

b. shelf   _____   e. thief   _____

c. half   _____   f. wolf   _____

a. wolves
b. leaves
c. halves
d. thieves
e. elves
f. shelves

26. To remember these particular words, let us put them in a context. Read the sentence first, then supply the plural form.

a. Every night _____ roam the countryside.
                    wolf

b. In the fall trees shed their _____.
                                    leaf

c. Jack cut the apples into _____.
                                half

d. The basement was broken into by _____.
                                        thief

e. Medieval folklore is filled with stories of _____.
elf

f. The clerk filled the _____.
shelf

lives
wives
knives

27. *Life*, *wife*, and *knife* are treated like the previous exceptions. How would you write the plurals of
life _____   wife _____   knife _____.

wives
lives
thieves
knives

28. Supply the plural forms.
The _____ fled for their _____ when
wife   life
the _____ came after them with _____.
thief   knife

a. mischiefs
b. halves
c. wives
d. cliffs
e. leaves
f. griefs
g. lives
h. gulfs
i. strifes
j. proofs
k. sheriffs
l. thieves
m. knives
n. elves

29. Write the plurals of these words.

a. mischief _____   h. gulf   _____

b. half   _____   i. strife   _____

c. wife   _____   j. proof   _____

d. cliff   _____   k. sheriff   _____

e. leaf   _____   l. thief   _____

f. grief   _____   m. knife   _____

g. life   _____   n. elf   _____

elf   elves
shelf   shelves
half   halves
leaf   leaves
thief   thieves
wolf   wolves
life   lives
wife   wives
knife   knives

30. You have studied nine words ending in f or fe that are exceptions to the general rule of adding s to form the plural. Write these nine words and then write their plurals. Here is *elf* as a starter.
elf _____   _____
     _____   _____
     _____   _____
     _____

bacteria
media
addenda

analyses
synopses
hypotheses

31. Some nouns, Latin in origin, take the Latin plural endings. For instance, words ending in *um*, like *datum*, take *a* to form the plural: *data*. Words ending in *is*, like *crisis*, take *es* to form the plural: *crises*.
Pick out the words in this list that take the plural *a* ending and write the plurals.

bacterium _____   medium   _____

analysis _____   hypothesis _____

synopsis _____   addendum _____

What are the plurals for these words:

analysis   _____   synopsis   _____

hypothesis _____

a. crises
b. data
hypotheses
c. analyses
d. parentheses
e. media

32. Supply the correct plural forms.

a. Almost every adult has had several _____ in

                                         crisis

his life.

b. The educator stated that the students had not presented sufficient _____ to prove their _____.

                               datum   hypothesis

c. Three scientists made separate _____

                                      analysis

of the new theory.

d. The two curved marks that indicate an inserted word
in a sentence are _____.

                                   parenthesis

e. The proprietor agreed to use all the _____ of

                                      medium

advertising.

REVIEW

s s s

33. What is the plural ending for most nouns ending in
o? _____ in *fe*? _____ in *ff*? _____

a. pianos
b. beliefs
c. wives
d. potatoes
e. zoos
f. autos
g. halves
h. radios
i. Negroes
j. heroes
k. cliffs
l. griefs
m. vetoes
n. thieves
o. tariffs

34. Test your skill by writing the plurals of these nouns.

a. piano _____   i. Negro _____

b. belief _____   j. hero _____

c. wife _____   k. cliff _____

d. potato _____   l. grief _____

e. zoo _____   m. veto _____

f. auto _____   n. thief _____

g. half _____   o. tariff _____

h. radio _____

a. wish
b. potato
c. half
d. hero
e. photo
f. thief
g. kangaroo
h. life
i. Negro
j. echo

35. Write the singular form of the following plurals.

a. wishes _____   f. thieves _____

b. potatoes _____   g. kangaroos _____

c. halves _____   h. lives _____

d. heroes _____   i. Negroes _____

e. photos _____   j. echoes _____

a. hypotheses
b. bacteria
c. oases
d. media
e. bases
f. data
g. addenda
h. analyses

36. Write the plurals of these Latin words.

a. hypothesis _____   e. basis _____

b. bacterium _____   f. datum _____

c. oasis _____   g. addendum _____

d. medium _____   h. analysis _____

POSTTEST

Write the plural for these singular nouns.

1. life _____
2. switch _____
3. monarch _____
4. echo _____
5. analysis _____
6. gulch _____
7. stereo _____
8. country _____
9. shelf _____
10. addendum _____
11. photo _____
12. treaty _____
13. tomato _____
14. medium _____
15. Kennedy _____

16. company _____
17. bungalow _____
18. compress _____
19. crisis _____
20. fashion _____
21. datum _____
22. knife _____
23. deputy _____
24. family _____
25. Henry _____
26. epoch _____
27. Negro _____
28. hypothesis _____
29. lobby _____
30. wolf _____

Chapter 15

POSSESSIVES

The possessive form is an important part of spelling. And even though it has become permissible to eliminate the apostrophe or apostrophe s in some expressions, like "for consciences sake" or "at wits end," current usage still requires the use of the apostrophe in most cases of the possessive.

In working through this chapter you will recognize the singular and plural forms, apply the rules for ' or 's to a number of nouns, use the ' or 's in forming the possessives of compound nouns, distinguish between indefinite pronouns and the possessive form of the personal pronouns, and convert the possessive phrases to "of" phrases, deciding which phrases may be more euphonious. Lastly, you will become doubly aware of the possessive case and its use.

PRETEST

Write the correct form of the possessive for the nouns, compound nouns, and personal pronouns below.

1. Yesterday was the end of the _____ reign.

   king

2. Someone stole the _____ bicycles.

   boys

3. _____ catalog is not in print.

   Brannon and Butterworth
   (double ownership)

4. _____ poetry is fascinating.

   John Donne

5. The _____ reports are inaccurate.

   secretary and treasurer
   (single ownership)

6. All the _____ hats were red.
   women

7. They listened to _____ demands.
   each other

8. _____ reforms were mediocre.
   Louis the Thirteenth

9. The canary fluffed _____ feathers.
   it

10. It's strange that _____ ideas were accepted.
    nobody

11. I'm tired of listening to my _____ complaints.
    friend

12. Let me see your _____ painting.
    father-in-law

13. In the experiment a _____ delay can be crucial.
    minute

---

a. P
b. S
c. S
d. P
e. P
f. S
g. S
h. P.
· · · · · · · · · · · ·
a. 's
b. 's
c. '
d. 's
e. '
f. '
g. 's
h. 's
i. '
j. 's

1. To form the possessive we use either the apostrophe (') or the apostrophe s ('s) and the rules are simple: **to** nouns *not* ending in s you add 's; to plural nouns ending in s you add '. Indicate by S or P whether the following are singular or plural.

a. mice _____   e. Marys _____

b. man _____   f. boy _____

c. Harry _____   g. woman _____

d. brothers _____   h. Joneses _____

· ·

Indicate which form each word takes: ' or 's.

a. woman _____   f. poets _____

b. cook _____   g. women _____

c. sopranos _____   h. alto _____

d. children _____   i. queens _____

e. Baileys _____   j. Mary _____

---

a. boy's
b. tables'
c. Charles'
d. women's
e. sisters'
f. uncle's
g. friends'
h. citizen's

2. Now write the complete possessive form for these nouns.

a. boy _____   e. sisters _____

b. tables _____   f. uncle _____

c. Charles _____   g. friends _____

d. women _____   h. citizen _____

's
'

a. Harry's
b. Adams'
c. Frost's
d. students'
e. queen's
f. Joneses'
g. women's
h. church's

3. To form the possessive of nouns not ending in *s* you add _____; to plural nouns ending in *s* you add _____.

4. Read each sentence carefully, then supply the correct possessive.

a. Put _____ coat on the chair.
         Harry

b. Tom _____ name was called first.
         Adams

c. Although I like John Keats' poetry, I prefer Robert _____.
   Frost

d. The _____ musical program was
         students
exceptional.

e. The _____ embroidered handkerchief is
         queen
missing.

f. The _____ farm is for sale.
         Joneses

g. Put the _____ names in a separate list.
             women

h. The _____ spire towered above the other
         church
buildings.

a. P
b. P
c. I
d. P
e. I
f. I   P

5. Indefinite pronouns also take ' or 's for the possessive: *one's* belief, *another's* ideas, or the *others'* receipts. But the possessive forms of the personal pronoun never include the apostrophe: *his, hers, its, ours, yours, theirs.* Indicate by I or P whether the underlined are indefinite or possessive personal pronouns.

a. The bird preened its feathers. _____
b. I'll bring my records if you bring yours. _____
c. Somebody's hat is on the table. _____
d. I've already had my turn; how it's hers. _____
e. Nobody's suggestions were accepted. _____
f. The others' proposals were illogical; ours were not.

_____   _____

a. everybody's
b. hers
c. its

6. Now write the correct possessives for these sentences.

a. Don't believe _____ statements.
                everybody

d. others'
e. theirs
f. anybody's
g. another's

b. This is _____.

her

c. The hawk eyed _____ prey.

it

d. The _____ proposals are innovative.

others

e. The property is _____.

their

f. It's _____ guess.

anybody

g. Many times one man's opinion is as good as _____.

another

a. its
b. it's
c. It's
d. its

7. Remember that the contraction *it's* stands for *it is*, and that the apostrophe takes the place of the *i* in *is*. This contraction is never substituted for the possessive form of the personal pronoun. Read each sentence carefully and write the correct form: *its, it's*.

a. The dog lay on _____ back for hours.

b. I keep forgetting that _____ Monday.

c. _____ almost five o'clock.

d. Why does the tiger keep licking _____ paw?

a. law
b. secretary
   treasurer
c. lantern
d. by
e. Numeier

8. To form the possessive of a compound noun (two or more words joined together to form a single noun), you add ' or 's to the last element of the compound noun. For example, the 's would be added to *law* in *father-in-law*. In a compound expression (two or more nouns joined by a conjunction, like *Sears and Roebuck*), you add the ' or 's to the last noun to show *double* ownership (they own it together): Sears and Roebuck's catalog. For *single* ownership (each owns a share) you add ' or 's to each noun: *Mary's* and *James'* reports on ecology.
Identify the part of the underlined compound nouns or expressions that require the possessive.

a. her sister-in-law cottage _____

b. the secretary and the treasurer reports _____

(single ownership)

c. the jack-o-lantern light _____

d. the passer-by shouts _____

e. Dunn and Numeier property _____

(double ownership)

a. somebody else's
b. Diller and Dollar's
c. brother-in-law's
d. secretary-
   treasurer's
e. runner-up's
f. Jim's and Jean's

9. For each sentence write the complete expression in the possessive form.

a. That book is _____.
                              somebody else

b. Today I received _____
                              Diller and Dollar
                              (double ownership)

seed catalog.

c. She hung her _____
                              brother-in-law

coat on the rack.

d. We listened attentively to the _____
                              secretary-treasurer
                              (double ownership)

report.

e. For a while the judge could not find the _____
                              runner-up

medal.

f. We went to _____
                              Jim and Jean
                              (single ownership)

cafe for lunch.

a. the coat of
   Mr. Adams
b. the legs of
   the chairs
c. the dome of
   the temple
d. the coats of
   the children
e. the keys of
   the piano
f. the property
   of the Kellys
• • • • • • • • • • • • •
Your choice, but prob-
ably the legs of the
chairs, the dome of
the temple, and the
keys of the piano—
the last two particu-
larly

10. Possession can be shown by an "of" phrase as well as by the apostrophe. Although either is correct, sometimes the phrase is not only easier to use but it sounds better. For example, *the book's pages* can be expressed *the pages of the book*, and in context the second phrase may sound more euphonious than the first.
Change these possessives to phrases, watching your singular and plural forms as you do.

a. Mr. Adams' coat   _____

b. the chairs' legs   _____

c. the temple's dome   _____

d. the children's coats   _____

e. the piano's keys   _____

f.   the Kellys' property   _____
• •
Which phrases you just wrote might sound better than the possessive with the apostrophe? _____

a. the semaphore's lights
b. the fans' blades
c. Tom Brown's glasses
d. the room's windows
e. the knife's edge
f. someone's proposal

• • • • • • • • • • • •
Your choice, again. You will probably agree that at least c. and f. sound better as possessives .

11. Now convert these "of" phrases to the possessive form.

a. the lights of the semaphore _____

b. the blades of the fans _____

c. the glasses of Tom Brown _____

d. the windows of the room _____

e. the edge of the knife _____

f. the proposal of someone _____

• •
Which "of" phrase(s) do you think sound better than the possessive(s)? _____

REVIEW

a. employee's
b. Adams'
c. Secretary of Development's
d. Tim's and Tena's
e. Williams'
f. mother-in-law's
g. people's
h. its
i. mayor's and governor's
j. bosses'
k. theirs
l. Smith and Butler's

12. Now test your skill in forming possessives.

a. The supervisor criticized the _____
employee

work.

b. A fence separates our property from the _____.
Adams

c. I doubt the veracity of the _____
Secretary of Development

statement.

d. _____ variety store
Tim and Tina
(single ownership)

closed Monday.

e. Joe _____ house is on the lakeshore.
Williams

f. I am using my _____
mother-in-law

drapes.

g. He is a staunch advocate of a _____
people

government.

h. The spider lured _____ prey into the web.
it

i. How many of the _____
mayor and governor
(single ownership)

reports do you have?

j. Both secretaries are complaining about their _____

bosses

strict rules.

k. John placed his hat on the chair; Jerry and Jim hung
_____ on the rack.

their

l. Let's have supper at _____

Smith and Butler
(double ownership)

drugstore.

POSTTEST

Test your skill by writing the correct possessive forms.

1. Tell Mary to put _____ on the table.

her

2. The chairman listened to the _____ opinions.

others

3. From around the corner came my _____ car.

niece

4. The council did not approve _____ suggestions.

anyone

5. It was difficult to listen to the _____ high notes.

sopranos

6. Let's go to _____ restaurant for dinner.

Day and May
(double ownership)

7. Are those your _____ overshoes?

sisters

8. Tell them to put _____ in front.

their

9. The bear guarded _____ cubs.

it

10. The _____ medal was 14-carat gold.

runner-up

11. Hanging on the wall were the _____ pictures.

actresses

12. Gray was the color selected for the _____ hats.

men

13. Is this _____ manuscript?
       Mary

14. Did you ask to use your _____ mower?
                                brother-in-law

15. The assembly heard _____ reports on pollution.
                          Jack and Jim
                          (single ownership)

Chapter 16

LY AND OUS

Do you often wonder whether to add *ly* or *ally*, and whether to change the ending of a word before adding *ous*? You need not wonder any longer, because Chapter 16 will present a few easy rules for you to follow. In this chapter you will (1) distinguish between words that take *ly* or *ally*; (2) recognize those words whose last letter must be kept, dropped, or changed before *ly* or *ous*; (3) recognize the exceptions to these rules; (4) state the reasons why pronunciation can be important in adding *ly* or *ous*; and (5) spell correctly a number of useful words in and out of context. By the end of the chapter you will be spelling such words as *publicly*, *truly*, *angrily*, *mischievous*, and *advantageous* correctly and confidently.

PRETEST

Choose the correct ending and write the complete word.

A. *ly-ally*

1. basic_____
2. moral_____
3. true_____
4. frequent_____
5. continuous_____
6. public_____
7. accidental_____
8. angry_____
9. chief_____
10. due_____
11. final_____
12. accurate_____
13. vague_____
14. whole_____
15. easy_____
16. coy_____
17. dry_____
18. safe_____
19. simple_____
20. sly_____

Add the suffix and write the complete word.

B. ous

21. vary_____	27. mountain_____
22. peril_____	28. adventure_____
23. advantage_____	29. trouble_____
24. mischief_____	30. grief_____
25. libel_____	31. victory_____
26. pity_____	32. space_____

LY-ALLY

finally

1. The general rule about forming an adverb with the suffix *ly* is to simply add *ly* after the root word. For example, *month + ly = monthly*.
Combine the root *final* and *ly*: _____.

a. frequently
b. morally
c. really
d. certainly
e. cruelly
f. accidentally
g. continuously
h. chiefly

2. Apply the rule to these roots.

a. frequent	_____	e. cruel	_____
b. moral	_____	f. accidental	_____
c. real	_____	g. continuous	_____
d. certain	_____	h. chief	_____

no—you were right
not to drop it

3. Several of the above adjectives end in the consonant *l*. Before adding *ly* did you drop the *l* at the end of the root?

_____

a. scarcely
b. duly
c. sparsely
d. truly
e. wholly
f. genuinely
g. crudely
h. simply

4. Some adjectives end in a silent e (an e that is not pronounced). Take the word *accurate* (the last sound is *t*). In adding *ly* you keep the e: *accurately*. There are four silent e words that do not keep the e: *due, true, whole,* and *simple*. Now add the suffix *ly* to the eight words below.

a. scarce	_____	e. whole	_____
b. due	_____	f. genuine	_____
c. sparse	_____	g. crude	_____
d. true	_____	h. simple	_____

whole
due
simple
true

5. From this list choose the words that drop the e before *ly*.

large	vague	simple
whole	like	true
safe	due	nice

duly
wholly
simply
truly

a. b. d. f.
• • • • • • • • • • • •
easily
hungrily
temporarily
trickily
• • • • • • • • • • • • •
coyly slyly

6. Add *ly* to the four exceptions and write the complete words.

_____   _____

_____   _____

7. Some words ending in *y* keep the *y* before *ly* and some do not. Pronounce the word *happy*. The *y* here has a long e sound (hap pee). Now pronounce the word *coy*. Here you do not have a long e sound, but a dipthong, *oy*. If a word ending in *y* has the long e sound, you drop the *y* and change it to *i* before adding *ly*: *happy* + *ly* = *happily*. If not, then you keep the *y*: *coy* + *ly* = *coyly*.
Identify which words have the long e sound of *y*:

a. easy _____   d. temporary _____

b. hungry _____   e. coy _____

c. sly _____   f. tricky _____

• •
Write the *ly* adverbs for easy _____, hungry

_____, temporary _____,

tricky _____.

• •
Write the *ly* adverbs for *coy* and *sly*. _____ _____

dryly or drily
shyly or shily

8. According to the rule *dry* and *shy* do not drop the *y* (they do not have the long sound of e). Modern usage, however, permits an alternative spelling; in other words, you would change the *y* to *i* before adding *ly*.
Write the two correct spellings of both words: _____

_____   _____   _____.

dry
shy

9. Name the two words that can be written with *y* or *i* before the *ly*: _____ _____

The *y* in each word
has a long e sound.
The *y* in both words
has a long i sound,
not a long e sound.

10. The words *hungry* and *angry* change the *y* to *i* before the *ly*. Why? _____
The words *wry* and *sly* retain the *y* before the *ly*. Why?
_____

REVIEW

a. tastily
b. finally
c. extremely
d. slyly
e. wholly
f. equally

11. Test your skill in forming *ly* adverbs.

a. tasty _____   d. sly _____

b. final _____   e. whole _____

c. extreme _____   f. equal _____

g. coyly
h. duly
i. unusually
j. dryly or drily
k. truly
l. entirely
m. morally
n. gorgeously
o. simply
p. easily

comfortably
conceivably
profitably

laughably
perceptibly

change the e to y

ally ally
ally ly

a. critically
b. automatically
c. specifically
d. drastically
e. publicly

g. coy _____
h. due _____
i. unusual _____
j. dry _____
k. true _____

l. entire _____
m. moral _____
n. gorgeous _____
o. simple _____
p. easy _____

12. Adjectives ending in *ble* (like *considerable*) already have the *l* in the last syllable. To form the adverb, just change the e to y. Considerable becomes considerably. What would be the adverbs for these "ble" words?

comfortable _____

conceivable _____

profitable _____

13. These adjectives also end in *ble*: *laughable* and *perceptible*. What are the *ly* adverbs? _____

_____

14. To form the *ly* adverb from an adjective ending in *ble*, what do you do? _____

15. To most adjectives ending in *ic* you must add *ally* instead of *ly*. To form the adverb from the adjective *basic* you add *ally*: *basically*. The *one* exception is the word *public*—it takes *ly*.
What is the correct suffix for each of these words (*ly, ally*)?

academic _____   genetic _____

automatic _____   public _____

16. Now form the adverbs by adding either *ly* or *ally*.

a. He is _____ ill.
        critic

b. She moved each object _____.
                    automatic

c. The proposal benefits each side _____.
                        specific

d. The woman reacted _____.
                drastic

e. He announced his intentions _____.
                    public

REVIEW

17. Add *ly* or *ally* as appropriate.

a. advisably
b. considerably
c. sensibly
d. basically
e. responsibly
f. publicly
g. automatically
h. reliably
i. terribly
j. apologetically
k. irritably
l. probably

a. advisable _____   g. automatic _____

b. considerable _____   h. reliable _____

c. sensible _____   i. terrible _____

d. basic _____   j. apologetic _____

e. responsible _____   k. irritable _____

f. public _____   l. probable _____

ally

18. Most words ending in *ic* add (*ly*, *ally*). _____

public

19. What one word ending in *ic* adds *ly*? _____

whole simple
due true

20. Most words ending in silent *e* simply add *ly* to the root. Four words are exceptions: _____ _____
_____ _____.

hungrily
y is preceded by a
consonant, so y is
changed to i; the y
has the long sound
of e

21. Choose the correct spelling and then state your reasons for this choice: hungryly hungrily. _____

OUS

e. g.

22. Most words ending in a consonant add *ous* to form the adjective meaning full of. To the word *marvel* (which ends in the consonant *l*) you add *ous*: *marvelous*. If words end in the consonant *f*, however, you change the *f* to *v* before the *ous*. For instance, the word *grief* becomes *grievous*. Now from this list identify the words whose last consonant must be changed to *v* before adding *ous*:

a. humor _____   e. mischief _____

b. peril _____   f. hazard _____

c. danger _____   g. grief _____

d. riot _____   h. mountain _____

a. humorous
b. perilous
c. dangerous
d. riotous
e. mischievous
f. hazardous
g. grievous
h. mountainous

a. desirous
b. outrageous
c. spacious
d. adventurous
e. troublous
f. gracious

23. Add *ous* to all the words in the preceding frame.

a. _____   e. _____

b. _____   f. _____

c. _____   g. _____

d. _____   h. _____

24. Now look at and pronounce these words:

    continue   advantage   space

All end in a silent *e*, but the second ends in *ge* and the third in *ce*. Both the *g* and *c* have the soft sound (as in *city* and *gem*). Generally, words ending in silent *e* drop the *e* before a suffix beginning with a vowel, so before adding *ous* to a word like *continue*, you would drop the *e*: *continuous*. With *advantage*, you must preserve the soft sound of *g* by keeping the *e*: *advantageous*. Otherwise you would get the hard sound of *g* as in "advantag ous." The soft sound of *c* presents a slightly different problem. Here you must change the *e* in *space*, for example, to *i*, not only to preserve the soft sound but also the pronunciation of the last syllable: "shus" in *spacious*. If you keep the *e* you would have to pronounce the word like this: spa   ce ous, which, of course, is wrong.
Here are six words. Apply these guidelines and add *ous* correctly to them.

a. desire _____   d. adventure _____

b. outrage _____   e. trouble _____

c. space _____   f. grace _____

a. grievous
b. poisonous
c. courageous
d. libelous
e. continuous
f. spacious
g. marvelous
h. mischievous

25. Now add *ous* to this list of words.

a. grief _____   e. continue _____

b. poison _____   f. space _____

c. courage _____   g. marvel _____

d. libel _____   h. mischief _____

26. Let us look at these words:

    vary   beauty

Both end in *y*, with a consonant preceding it: an *r* in *vary* and a *t* in *beauty*. When you add a suffix beginning with a vowel, like *ous*, to words ending in *y* preceded by a consonant you usually change the *y* to *i*. *Vary* follows this rule: *various*. You cannot change the *y* in beauty to *i*, however,

a. victorious
b. plenteous
c. injurious
d. piteous

because you will change the pronunciation. The sound of the *y* is a long e (beautee), and to keep that sound you must change the *y* to e: *beauteous*. Changing the *y* to *i* would change the last syllable to "tious" (or "shus"), which, of course, would be wrong.
Add *ous* to these words.

a. victory _____   c. injury _____

b. plenty _____   d. pity _____

e
i

27. So as not to get the "shus" sound in pit___ous, you drop the *y* from *pity* and add _____. On the other hand, to keep the "shus" sound in spac___ous, you change the e to _____ and then add *ous*.

t

28. Before adding *ous* to words ending in a final *y*, check to see which consonant precedes the *y*. Change the *y* to e if the consonant is _____.

a. spacious
b. piteous
c. gracious

29. Add *ous* to these roots and write the complete words.

a. space _____   c. grace _____

b. pity _____

REVIEW

a. ridiculous
b. vigorous
c. gracious
d. courageous
e. mountainous
f. desirous
g. various
h. grievous
i. plenteous
j. dangerous
k. spacious
l. bounteous
m. mischievous
n. riotous
o. advantageous
p. porous

30. Now test your skill by adding *ous* to these words and writing the complete words.

a. ridicule _____   i. plenty _____

b. vigor _____   j. danger _____

c. grace _____   k. space _____

d. courage _____   l. bounty _____

e. mountain _____   m. mischief _____

f. desire _____   n. riot _____

g. vary _____   o. advantage _____

h. grief _____   p. pore _____

drop

31. In adding *ous* to *desire*, you (drop, keep) the e. _____

keep
e retains soft g.

32. In adding *ous* to *advantage*, or *courage*, you (drop, keep) the silent e. _____
State the reason why. _____

i

33. *Space* and *grace* have a soft *c*. But instead of keeping the e, you must change it to ＿＿ before *ous*.

v

34. Words ending in *f* change the *f* to ＿＿ before *ous*.

e

35. The following words end in a long e sound: *plenty, bounty, pity*. So that this sound is not changed before *ous*, you must drop the y and add ＿＿.

POSTTEST

Add the suffix to the root word and write the complete word.

A. *ly-ally*

1. real ＿＿＿＿＿＿＿＿＿

11. academic ＿＿＿＿＿＿＿＿＿

2. angry ＿＿＿＿＿＿＿＿＿

12. entire ＿＿＿＿＿＿＿＿＿

3. true ＿＿＿＿＿＿＿＿＿

13. simple ＿＿＿＿＿＿＿＿＿

4. shy ＿＿＿＿＿＿＿＿＿

14. like ＿＿＿＿＿＿＿＿＿

5. certain ＿＿＿＿＿＿＿＿＿

15. tasty ＿＿＿＿＿＿＿＿＿

6. final ＿＿＿＿＿＿＿＿＿

16. perceptible ＿＿＿＿＿＿＿＿＿

7. public ＿＿＿＿＿＿＿＿＿

17. drastic ＿＿＿＿＿＿＿＿＿

8. hungry ＿＿＿＿＿＿＿＿＿

18. due ＿＿＿＿＿＿＿＿＿

9. apologetic ＿＿＿＿＿＿＿＿＿

19. tricky ＿＿＿＿＿＿＿＿＿

10. whole ＿＿＿＿＿＿＿＿＿

20. sly ＿＿＿＿＿＿＿＿＿

B. *ous*

21. grief ＿＿＿＿＿＿＿＿＿

27. ridicule ＿＿＿＿＿＿＿＿＿

22. desire ＿＿＿＿＿＿＿＿＿

28. bounty ＿＿＿＿＿＿＿＿＿

23. hazard ＿＿＿＿＿＿＿＿＿

29. danger ＿＿＿＿＿＿＿＿＿

24. courage ＿＿＿＿＿＿＿＿＿

30. riot ＿＿＿＿＿＿＿＿＿

25. grace ＿＿＿＿＿＿＿＿＿

31. injury ＿＿＿＿＿＿＿＿＿

26. plenty ＿＿＿＿＿＿＿＿＿

32. mischief ＿＿＿＿＿＿＿＿＿

Appendixes

Appendix A

GUIDELINES FOR SYLLABICATION

To be correctly spelled, some words seem to defy rules, pronunciation or meaning guides, and about the only way to master them is to divide them into syllables. This does not mean that only these words should be syllabified; on the contrary, syllabication is a good basis for spelling many words, particularly unfamiliar ones.

Of the several methods of syllabication the one presented here is a graphic presentation, not a phonetic one. Not that sound is unimportant. Indeed it is, but to give you a phonetic system without being able to assume that you have studied linguistics would be assuming too much. The graphic system does take pronunciation and the various characteristics of the English language into account, and since it demands some knowledge of vowel sounds, stress, and the components of words, this chapter will present this basic material as concisely as possible. You will become familiar with long and short sounds of vowels, semivowels, dipthongs, and the stress in syllables. Further, you will apply specific guidelines in the dividing of words of two or more syllables. By the end of the appendix you will confidently divide a word into its parts. One last word: these guidelines are simply that. They are not hard and fast rules, but aids. They will, however, help you to spell correctly and to follow the syllabication in any standard dictionary. If you already know about vowels, consonants, dipthongs, stress, and the like, you can begin with frame 13. If you are unfamiliar with this material, or if you want a short refresher, start at the beginning of the chapter.

PRETEST

Divide these words into syllables. To indicate the separation between syllables, leave a space in between: con   fer   ence.

1. necessary _____
2. manufacture _____
3. vowel _____
4. accommodate _____
5. carpenter _____
6. rapid _____
7. consideration _____
8. antipathy _____
9. geology _____
10. rubble _____

11. reference _____
12. accumulate _____
13. delude _____
14. pilot _____
15. sophomore _____
16. antibody _____
17. consonant _____
18. appearance _____
19. tribulation _____
20. rivalry _____

---

a. C
b. C
c. C
d. S
e. S
f. V
g. C
h. V

1. Of the twenty-six letters of the English alphabet five can be classed as vowels, three as semivowels, and the rest as consonants. The vowel sounds are represented by the letters *a, e, i, o, u*; the semivowels *w, h, y*; and the consonants by the other letters, like *b, c, d, g, s.*
Indicate by V, S, or C whether the following letters represent vowels, semivowels, or consonants.

a. s_____   c. b_____   e. h_____   g. x_____
b. p_____   d. w_____   f. e_____   h. a_____

---

i   o   u

2. In the preceding frame you checked *a* and *e* as vowels. You were correct. Name the other three: _____

---

y

3. You checked *w* and *h* as semivowels, and again you were correct. What is the third semivowel? _____

---

a   e   i   o   u
w   h   y

4. List all the vowels and semivowels: _____
_____.

---

b.   d.   e.   g.   h.

5. Identify the consonants.

a. a_____   c. u_____   e. b_____   g. f_____
b. g_____   d. s_____   f. h_____   h. k_____

A.
· · · · · · · · · · · · · ·
yes

6. For the vowels there are long and short sounds and dipthongs. The long sounds are usually higher, longer, and tenser than the short sounds. Pronounce these words: *bite* and *bit.* Yes, the *i* in *bite* is higher, longer, and tenser than the *i* in *bit,* so it is the long sound. Since the *i* in *bit* is not nearly as long, high, or tense, it is the short sound. Dipthongs are speech sounds moving from one vowel to another vowel or to a semivowel within the same syllable. Take the words *boil* and *toy.* Pronounce them slowly—the vowels *oi* and the vowel *o* and semivowel *y* blend together. Pronounce these two groups of words, then answer this question: Which group has the long sound of the vowels?

_____

A.	B.
Pete	bit
rate	top
beet	met
proof	hat
stone	but
night	knit
rude	rut

· ·

Do the underlined portions in these words qualify as dipthongs? _____

spout   plow

a. S
b. L
c. D
d. L
e. D
f. S

7. Now identify whether the underlined portions are long or short vowels, or dipthongs. Use L, S, or D as indicators.

a. bitter _____   d. frame _____

b. key _____   e. pout _____

c. boil _____   f. butter _____

8. Sometimes two vowel letters result in a long vowel sound. To distinguish between the long vowel and the dipthong remember that a long sound is *one* sound, whereas a dipthong is a *movement* from one vowel sound to another or to a semivowel. Here are two words: *freight* and *mate.* Both have the long *a* sound. In the first, two vowels (ei) constitute the single sound; in the second, the single vowel *a.* In the words *toil* (two vowels) or *boy* (vowel and semivowel) you have dipthongs as there is a movement from *o* to *i* and from *o* to *y.*

a. L
b. D
c. L
d. L
e. L
f. D
g. L
h. D

Pronounce each word below, then identify whether the underlined portion is a long sound (L) or a dipthong (D).

a. believe	_____	e. meat	_____
b. boisterous	_____	f. poise	_____
c. boat	_____	g. main	_____
d. reindeer	_____	h. plow	_____

a. C
b. V
c. C
d. V
e. D
f. V
g. C
h. D

9. The *semi* in semivowel suggests that they are and they are not vowels. This is correct because in most systems of classification w, h, and y are included with the consonants but are acknowledged as being capable of producing vowel sounds. As consonants they precede vowels, as in way, you, and he; as vowels they usually follow a simple vowel to help make a long vowel sound: tow, or a dipthong: ploy. The y can also be a full vowel with the long sound of e. If you pronounce *skinny* or *clammy*, you will hear the long e sound of y; its function, of course, is to serve as a suffix (or ending).

Now check which sound the underlined portions produce: C (consonant), V (vowel), and D (dipthong).

a. hoe	_____	e. boy	_____
b. lawyer	_____	f. they	_____
c. wide	_____	g. yea	_____
d. low	_____	h. cow	_____

long e
suffix (or ending)

10. Now pronounce these words:

gossipy   chunky   happy

What sound does the y have? _____

What is the function of the y? _____

11. There are several technical ways to define a syllable and its components, but suffice it to say that a syllable is the smallest phonological construction and usually consists of a pronounced vowel or dipthong or either one or more vowels with one or more consonants. Let us also say that a syllable can form a complete word or is part of a larger word. For instance, the word *bat* has one pronounced vowel (a) which is preceded by and followed by one consonant (b and t). The sounds produce just one syllable, in this case a complete word. Often such a word is called a one-syllable word. Now take the word *plow*— it has a dipthong instead of a single vowel—but together with the consonants pl it forms one syllable, and again a complete word. If you add a suffix to a word, like er to

a. 2
b. 3
c. 1
d. 2
e. 2
f. 5
g. 1
h. 3
i. 2

bat, you get *batter*. Here you have two pronounced vowels (*a* and *e*) forming two syllables: bat ter. Root words, those words without any additions (prefixes or suffixes), can have more than one syllable, for example: *garden, cloister, establish.* In each word you have several pronounced vowels or diphthongs: gar den clois ter es tab lish. Sometimes a consonant can form a syllable without a vowel (called a syllabic consonant). Pronounce these words: *riddle, bottle.* Each has two syllables *rid dle bot tle,* with the second syllable having just an "l" sound. In summing up, we can say that a syllable consists of either a vowel or a dipthong alone, a syllabic consonant, or either one or the other with one or more consonants. Now say the following words carefully, looking at and hearing the vowels. Then indicate the number of syllables in each.

a. summer _____   f. considerable _____

b. consonant _____   g. coat _____

c. hoe _____   h. disapprove _____

d. vowel _____   i. battle _____

e. shepherd _____

a. clámmy
b. repeĺ
c. none
d. accoḿmodate
e. páddle
f. cońsonant
g. preseŕve
h. none

12. One last point to consider before studying the guidelines is the stress. Stress (or accent) is the prominence which develops from pronouncing one or more syllables more strongly than the other(s). Since one-syllable words have no stress, let us turn to multisyllabic words. *Garden,* for instance, has two syllables and in pronouncing it you stress the first syllable: gaŕ den. In *establish* you stress the second: es tab́ lish. In the word *consideration,* however, you have more than one stress resulting in what we call "major" (´) and "minor" (´) stress: con sid́ er á tion. But remember, there is never more than one major stress in a word.

Now indicate the stress or stresses in these words. Use the same marks shown above: the bold mark for major, a similar but lighter mark for minor. If the word has no accent indicate "none."

a. clammy _____   e. paddle _____

b. repel _____   f. consonant _____

c. course _____   g. preserve _____

d. accommodate _____   h. club _____

a. vowels
b. long
c. is

13. Now we are ready for the guidelines. If a single consonant comes between two vowels, the first of which has a *long* sound and is *accented*, the consonant will usually go with the *second* vowel. Look at and pronounce *pilot*. The single consonant *l* comes between two vowels *i* and *o*. The first vowel has the long sound of *i* and carries the stress (pí lot). The consonant *l* will therefore go with the second vowel: pi lot. Now pronounce the word *garden*. It has the stress on the first vowel, but between the two vowels (*a* and *e*) come two consonants (*r* and *d*). We cannot apply this guideline to this word. How about *money*? Again we have two vowels (*o* and *e*) and a single consonant (*n*) between the two vowels, but the first vowel (*o*) does not have the long sound. So this word cannot be divided like pilot. To divide words like pilot we must look for these requirements:

a. it must have a single consonant between two _____.

b. the first vowel must have a (long, short) sound. _____

c. the first vowel (is, is not) stressed. _____

a. no
b. yes
c. no
d. yes
e. no
f. no

14. For each two-syllable word below, write yes or no to indicate whether it would be divided like pilot.

a. compel _____   d. local _____

b. native _____   e. rusty _____

c. polish _____   f. palace _____

a. 1 and 2
b. 3
c. 1 and 3
d. 3

15. *Native* and *local* are syllabified like pilot as they meet all the requirements. For the rest of the words in the above list, write the number of the reason(s) for their not meeting the requirements.
1. two consonants between two vowels
2. stress on second syllable
3. short sound of first vowel
4. a vowel between two consonants

a. compel _____   c. rusty _____

b. polish _____   d. palace _____

a. fi   nal
b. na   tive
c. lo   cal
d. ri   val
e. fa   vor

16. Now divide these words into syllables, leaving a space to indicate the separation: pi lot.

a. final _____   d. rival _____

b. native _____   e. favor _____

c. local _____

do

17. We are ready for the second guideline: when a consonant comes between vowels, the first of which is *short* and
accented, the consonant will usually go with the *first*
vowel. *Modest* is a good example. The *d* comes between
the *o* and *e,* the first vowel has a short sound of *o* and is
accented, so the *d* goes with the first vowel (*o*) to form
the first syllable: mod est. Pronounce these words:

          palace   solid   ravel   tepid

They (do, do not) meet this guideline. _____

a. pal   ace
b. sol   id
c. rav   el
d. tep   id

18. Now divide the following into syllables.

a. palace   _____   c. ravel   _____

b. solid   _____   d. tepid   _____

a. ro   bust
b. rap id
c. ten or
d. me   ter
e. mon ey
f. pu   pil
g. bo   nus
h. del uge

19. Test your skill by applying the guidelines presented
thus far to these words.

a. robust   _____   e. money   _____

b. rapid   _____   f. pupil   _____

c. tenor   _____   g. bonus   _____

d. meter   _____   h. deluge _____

a. pot   ter
b. jag   ged
c. pon   der
d. gos   sip
e. med   dle
f. hur   tle
g. car   pet
h. gin   ger

20. Here is the third guideline: if a word has two consonants between two vowels, you usually divide between the
consonants. For instance, in *garden* the *rd* comes between
a nd *e.* To divide you would separate the *r* and *d*: gar den.
If a word ends in *le* the consonant preceding the *le* usually
combines with the *le* to form a syllable. Take the word
turtle. It ends in *le,* so the consonant immediately preceding it (*t*) goes with the *le* to form the second syllable:
tur *tle.*
Keeping these guidelines in mind, divide the following:

a. potter   _____   e meddle   _____

b. jagged   _____   f. hurtle   _____

c. ponder   _____   g. carpet   _____

d. gossip   _____   h. ginger   _____

21. As far as possible try to syllabify a word according to
its structure, but always keep the pronunciation in mind.
If the word contains a prefix (an element added to the beginning of a word), and this prefix sounds out a syllable,
separate it from the root word: *dis* approve, *re* fer. Let us
look at these words: *misspell, disappoint, antibody.* Each
has a prefix (*mis, dis, anti*), so it can be separated from

a. pre fer
b. dis miss
c. pro ceed
d. dis ap pear
e. per form
f. an tith e sis

the root. But there is a difference: *mis* and *dis* have one syllable and *anti* has two. The proper syllabication then would be *mis* spell, *dis* ap point, *an ti bod y*. Here is another *anti*: *antipathy*. The prefix in this word is not pronounced the same as in *antibody*, so in *antipathy* the pronunciation must be followed for syllabication:

an ti bod y   but   an tip a thy

Say the following words aloud, then syllabify them.

a. prefer _____   d. disappear _____

b. dismiss _____   e. perform _____

c. proceed _____   f. antithesis _____

a. *ly*
b. *ness*
c. *ful* *ness*
d. *y*
e. *ence*

22. You should also be able to distinguish suffixes (elements at the end of words) from the roots. For instance, *helpful, entirely,* and *consolable* each have a suffix: *ful, ly,* and *able*. Again we have two (*ful* and *ly*) that have **one** syllable each, and *able* that has two.
For the following words identify the suffix in each **word**. Remember that words can have more than one suffix.

a. happily _____   d. grumpy _____

b. trueness _____   e. existence _____

c. helpfulness _____

a. hap pi ly
b. true ness
c. help ful ness
d. grump y
e. ex is tence

23. Let us take the same words in frame 22 to syllabify. You have identified the suffixes, so now, remembering your guidelines, pronounce the words carefully and write the syllables.

a. happily _____   d. grumpy _____

b. trueness _____   e. existence _____

c. helpfulness _____

2 consonants (*st*)
between 2 vowels
(*i* *e*)

24. Even though *existence* has a suffix (*ence*) why do you divide between the *st* for the second and third syllables:

_____

REVIEW

a. del uge
b. stu pid
c. por tal
d. dou ble
e. de lude
f. pos ture
g. re vise
h. doubt ful
i. stum ble
j. hub bub
k. jum bo

25. Test your skill by dividing these words into syllables. Remember that pronunciation and stress are important.

a. deluge ＿＿＿＿＿＿   g. revise ＿＿＿＿＿＿

b. stupid ＿＿＿＿＿＿   h. doubtful ＿＿＿＿＿＿

c. portal ＿＿＿＿＿＿   i. stumble ＿＿＿＿＿＿

d. double ＿＿＿＿＿＿   j. hubbub ＿＿＿＿＿＿

e. delude ＿＿＿＿＿＿   k. jumbo ＿＿＿＿＿＿

f. posture ＿＿＿＿＿＿

second

26. When a single consonant comes between two vowels, the first of which is long and accented (*local*) the consonant usually goes with the (first, second) vowel. ＿＿＿＿

first

27. When a single consonant comes between two vowels, the first of which is short and accented (*palace*), the consonant usually goes with the (first, second) vowel. ＿＿＿＿

le

28. If a word ends in *le*, the consonant preceding it goes with the ＿＿＿＿＿ to form a syllable.

between

29. If two consonants come between two vowels, you usually divide ＿＿＿＿＿＿ the consonants.

3
first
soph o more

30. Now that you have these guidelines firmly in mind, let us take longer words. How about *accommodate*. Since there are four pronounced vowels you can assume that there are four syllables. If you look closely at the word you will see two double consonants: *cc* and *mm*, both between vowels. You can divide between these double consonants: ac com modate. The last part can be divided after the long sound of *o* (in modate) and thus you have the four syllables: ac com mo date. The word *sophomore* is also a good word to syllabify. How many pronounced vowels does it have? ＿＿＿ Coming as it does from the Greek, it has the *ph* sounding like the single consonant *f*. Does the *ph* go with the first or second vowel? ＿＿＿＿＿ Now divide it into syllables. ＿＿＿＿＿＿＿

a. per fec tion
b. com mit tee
c. prep a ra tion
d. ar gu ment
e. suc ces sion
f. spec i men

31. Here are some multisyllabic words to divide. Pronounce them carefully and then apply the guidelines.

a. perfection ＿＿＿＿＿   d. argument ＿＿＿＿＿

b. committee ＿＿＿＿＿   e. succession ＿＿＿＿＿

c. preparation ＿＿＿＿＿   f. specimen ＿＿＿＿＿

a. car   pen   ter
b. es   tab   lish
   ment
c. dis   crim   i
   nate
d. lib   er   al
e. ac   cu   mu
   late
f. du   pli   cate
g. nec   es   sar   y
h. in   ef   fec   tive

32. Below is a list of questions to remind you of the guidelines for syllabication.
Is there a vowel between two consonants?
Is the first vowel long or short?
Are there two consonants between two vowels?
Is there a prefix or suffix in the word?
Does the word end in *le*?
Using these questions as reminders, divide the following words. Don't forget to pronounce them.

a. carpenter _____   e. accumulate _____

b. establishment _____   f. duplicate _____

c. discriminate _____   g. necessary _____

d. liberal _____   h. ineffective _____

POSTTEST

Divide these words into syllables. To indicate the separation, leave a space in between: gar   den   er.

1. controversy _____   11. incidental _____
2. restaurant _____   12. documentary _____
3. recurrence _____   13. knowledge _____
4. precede _____   14. Wednesday _____
5. disappointment _____   15. psychology _____
6. tremendous _____   16. ridiculous _____
7. unnecessary _____   17. achievement _____
8. description _____   18. forgotten _____
9. opportunity _____   19. government _____
10. advantageous _____   20. procedure _____

Appendix B

TEST ANSWERS

CHAPTER 1   PRONUNCIATION AND ENUNCIATION

PRETEST

1. hindrance	8. temperature	15. prejudice	22. environment
2. recognize	9. athletics	16. federal	23. background
3. athlete	10. liable	17. remembrance	24. gratitude
4. mischievous	11. finally	18. grievous	25. hundred
5. lightening	12. disastrous	19. temperament	26. aggravate
6. tragedy	13. vegetable	20. quantity	
7. chimney	14. lightning	21. government	

If you had 23 of 26 correct, you may bypass this chapter. But before you do, find your wrong answer numbers (if any) below, and read the corresponding frames in the chapter so that you will not misspell any words in this test.

Answer numbers	Frames	Answer numbers	Frames
1, 3, 4, 5, 7, 9, 12, 14, 17, 18	1–25	11, 20, 21, 22, 23	38–55
10, 16	27–34	2, 6, 15, 24, 25, 26	58–78
8, 13, 19	35–37		

POSTTEST

1. temperature	8. chimney	15. recognize	22. background
2. athlete	9. quantity	16. lightning	23. tragedy
3. grievous	10. liable	17. disastrous	24. finally
4. federal	11. temperament	18. mischievous	25. government
5. remembrance	12. hundred	19. athletics	26. gratitude
6. vegetable	13. aggravate	20. lightening	
7. environment	14. prejudice	21. hindrance	

For any wrong answers check the frames below and reread that part of the program. You do not want to leave this chapter without spelling every word correctly.

Answer numbers	Frames	Answer numbers	Frames
2. 3, 18, 19	1–7	9, 24	38–44
5, 17, 21	8–18	7, 22, 25	45–55
8, 16, 20	19–25	12, 13, 15, 26	58–73
4, 10	27–34	14, 23	74–78
1, 6, 11	35–37		

CHAPTER 2   PREFIXES

PRETEST

A.
1. disseminate
2. misspell
3. unnecessary
4. recollect
5. dissent

6. mistake
7. dissect
8. unnatural
9. recommend

B.
10. perform
11. prepare
12. dissatisfied
13. proceed
14. precede

15. decide
16. proscribe
17. describe
18. prescribe

If you spelled 16 of 18 correctly, you may bypass this chapter. But before you do, find your wrong answer numbers (if any) below and read the corresponding frames in the chapter so that you will not misspell any words in this test.

Answer numbers	Frames	Answer numbers	Frames
5, 12, 15, 17	1–4	4, 9	11–15
10, 11, 13, 14, 16, 18	5–8	1 2, 3, 6, 7, 8	16

POSTTEST

1. perspire
2. prescription
3. persuaded
4. despair
5. prefer

6. permeated
7. describe
8. proceed
9. dissect
10. permission

11. down
12. through
13. apart
14. back
15. through

16. not
17. off (or away)
18. before
19. away (or off)
20. not

For any wrong answers check the frame references below and reread that part of the program. You do not want to leave this chapter without spelling every word in the test correctly.

Answer numbers	Frames	Answer numbers	Frames
4, 7, 11, 13, 16, 17, 19, 20	1–4	14	11–15
1, 2, 3, 5, 6, 8, 10, 12, 15, 18	5–8	9	16

CHAPTER 3   SYLLABICATION

PRETEST

1. interest
2. embarrass
3. irrelevant
4. sergeant
5. villain
6. experience
7. acquire
8. immediately

9. dissatisfaction
10. vacuum
11. apparent
12. convenience
13. procedure
14. occasionally
15. disappoint
16. loneliness

17. opportunity
18. financier
19. discrimination
20. parallel
21. accumulate
22. disappear
23. interrupt
24. restaurant

25. appreciate
26. acquaintance
27. explanation
28. accomplishment
29. possession

If you had 26 of 29 correct, you may bypass this chapter. But before you do, find your wrong answer numbers, if any, below and read the corresponding frames in the chapter so that you will not misspell any words in this test.

Answer numbers	Frames	Answer numbers	Frames
11, 14, 17, 21, 25, 28	1–15	13, 27	57–61
9, 15, 19, 22	17–25	6, 12	63–71
2, 8, 20, 29	26–39	5	72–74
7, 26	41–44	1, 10	75–80
3, 16, 23	45–56	4, 18, 24	81–88

POSTTEST

1. vacuum	9. immediately	17. opportunity	25. explanation
2. villain	10. procedure	18. convenience	26. accomplishment
3. interest	11. occasionally	19. interrupt	27. parallel
4. sergeant	12. loneliness	20. acquaintance	28. possession
5. embarrass	13. financier	21. dissatisfaction	29. irrelevant
6. acquire	14. apparent	22. restaurant	
7. disappear	15. discrimination	23. appreciate	
8. experience	16. accumulate	24. disappoint	

For any wrong answer(s) check the frame references below and reread that part of the program. You do not want to leave this chapter without spelling every word in the test correctly.

Answer numbers	Frames	Answer numbers	Frames
11, 14, 16, 17, 23, 26	1–14	10, 25	57–61
7, 15, 21, 24	17–25	8, 18	63–71
5, 9, 27, 28	26–39	2	72–74
6, 20	41–44	1, 3	75–80
12, 19, 29	45–56	4, 13, 22	81–88

CHAPTER 4   SILENT LETTERS

PRETEST

1. Wednesday	5. psychology	9. exhaust	13. psychiatry
2. debt	6. rhythm	10. guard	14. doubt
3. condemn	7. knowledge	11. subtle	
4. guardian	8. undoubtedly	12. writer	

If you had 12 of 14 correct, you may bypass this chapter. But before you do, find any wrong answer numbers below, and read the corresponding frames in the chapter so that you will not misspell any word in this test.

Answer numbers	Frames	Answer numbers	Frames
2, 8, 11, 14	1–3	3	22–27
1	4–7	5, 13	28–32
6, 9	8–16	4, 10	33–36
7	17–20	12	37–41

POSTTEST

1. guard	5. Wednesday	9. condemn	13. exhaust
2. writing	6. rhythm	10. guardian	14. writer
3. psychology	7. knowledge	11. subtle	15. psychiatry
4. doubt	8. debt	12. undoubtedly	

For any wrong answer(s) check the frame references below and reread that part of the program. You do not want to leave this chapter without spelling every word in the test correctly.

Answer numbers	Frames	Answer numbers	Frames
4, 8, 11, 12	1–3	9	22–27
5	4–7	3, 15	28–32
6, 13	8–16	1, 10	33–36
7	17–20	2, 14	37–41

CHAPTER 5   VOWEL STRESS

PRETEST
1. benefit
2. grammar
3. optimism
4. familiar
5. humorous
6. comparative
7. ridiculous
8. eliminate
9. similar
10. dominant
11. warrant
12. candidate
13. sentence
14. mandatory
15. dormitory
16. mathematics
17. sacrifice
18. controversy
19. opinion
20. criticism
21. separate
22. definite
23. calendar
24. legitimate
25. category
26. divide
27. probably
28. fascinate
29. particular
30. privilege
31. laboratory
32. peculiar
33. bulletin
34. intelligence

If you had 30 of 34 correct, you may bypass this chapter. But before you do, find your wrong answers (if any) below, and read the corresponding frames in the chapter so that you will not misspell any words in this test.

Answer numbers	Frames	Answer numbers	Frames
7, 26	1–7	6, 14, 21, 27	31–41
11, 19, 29	8–17	1, 16, 25, 33	42–44
2, 9, 23	18–22	5, 18, 31	45–48
4, 32	23–26	3, 8, 10, 12, 15,	50–76
13	27–28	17, 20, 22, 24, 28,	
		30, 34	

POSTTEST
1. benefit
2. dormitory
3. opinion
4. sacrifice
5. peculiar
6. sentence
7. humorous
8. definite
9. criticism
10. warrant
11. laboratory
12. candidate
13. ridiculous
14. calendar
15. probably
16. bulletin
17. legitimate
18. mandatory
19. familiar
20. comparative
21. category
22. dominant
23. divide
24. grammar
25. mathematics
26. controversy
27. fascinate
28. optimism
29. separate
30. privilege
31. similar
32. particular
33. eliminate
34. intelligence

For any wrong answer(s) check the frame references below and reread that part of the program. You do not want to leave this chapter without spelling every word in the test correctly.

Answer numbers	Frames	Answer numbers	Frames
13, 23	1–7	7, 11, 26	45–48
3, 10, 32	8–17	8, 22	50–54
14, 24, 31	18–22	12, 17, 27, 33	55–62
5, 19	23–26	9, 28	63–67
6	27–28	2	68–70
15, 18, 20, 29	31–41	34	71–73
1, 16, 21, 25	42–44	4, 30	74–76

CHAPTER 6   SOUND-ALIKE SUFFIXES

PRETEST
A. *able-ible*
1. permissible
2. acceptable
3. estimable
4. changeable
5. admirable
6. marketable
7. inevitable
8. eligible
9. considerable
10. passable
11. possible
12. perishable
13. defensible
14. repressible
15. reducible
16. educable

B. *ary-ery*
1. boundary
2. stationery
3. secretary
4. library
5. cemetery
6. February
7. contemporary
8. stationary

C. *ise-ize-yze*
1. advise
2. analyze
3. criticize
4. summarize
5. surprise
6. emphasize
7. paralyze
8. exercise
9. advertise
10. realize

D. *ance-ence*
1. intelligent
2. resistance
3. equivalent
4. accident
5. defendant
6. prominence
7. existent
8. confidence
9. science
10. consequent
11. experience
12. magnificence
13. maintenance
14. excellent
15. guidance
16. influence
17. extravagance
18. insistent
19. attendance
20. dominant
21. prevalence
22. descendant
23. brilliance
24. significant

If you had 14 of 16 in A, 7 of 8 in B, 9 of 10 in C, and 21 of 24 in D correct, you may bypass this chapter. But before you do, find your wrong answer numbers (if any) below, and read the corresponding frames in the chapter so that you will not misspell any words in this test.

Answer numbers	Frames	Answer numbers	Frames
A.		C.	
2, 6, 9, 12	1	1, 5, 8, 9	43–51
3, 5	4–6	2, 7	52–56
7	7–8	3, 4, 6, 10	57–68
1, 10, 11, 14	9–10	D.	
13	12–14	2, 7, 18	70–73
4, 8, 15, 16	16–19	1, 12, 17, 24	74–76
B.		3, 6, 13, 14, 20, 21	78–80
2, 5	32–34	4, 5, 8, 15, 19, 22	82–84
8	35–36	9, 10, 11, 16, 23	85–88
1, 3, 4, 6, 7	36–37		

POSTTEST

A. *ary-ery*
1. contemporary
2. stationary
3. boundary
4. cemetery
5. February
6. secretary
7. library
8. stationery

B. *ise-ize-yze*
1. arise
2. supervise
3. characterize
4. analyze
5. surprise
6. recognize
7. advise
8. exercise
9. criticize
10. paralyze
11. realize
12. summarize

C. *able-ible*
1. multipliable
2. enforceable
3. perfectible
4. enjoyable
5. admissible
6. responsible
7. commendable
8. legible
9. corruptible
10. revocable
11. kissable
12. horrible
13. consolable
14. irritable
15. intelligible
16. dispensable

D. *ance-ence*
1. science
2. convenience
3. descendant
4. importance
5. dominance
6. extravagant
7. abundance
8. resistance
9. persistence
10. attendance
11. balance
12. adolescent

13. significance	16. defendant	19. excellence	22. guidance
14. delinquent	17. maintenance	20. brilliant	23. affluent
15. competent	18. relevant	21. permanent	24. emergence

For any wrong answer(s) check the frame references below and reread that part of the program. You do not want to leave this chapter without spelling every word in the test correctly.

Answer numbers	Frames	Answer numbers	Frames
A.		C.	
4, 8	32–34	7, 12	1
1, 3, 5, 6, 7	35–36	1, 4	2–3
2	36–37	3, 5, 9, 13, 14	4–6
		5, 11	9–11
B.		6, 16	12–14
1, 5, 8	43–48	2, 8, 10, 15	16–19
2, 7	49–51		
4, 10	52–56	D.	
11	57–60	4, 8, 9, 15, 18	70–73
6, 9	61–65	6, 12, 13, 24	74–76
3, 12	66–68	5, 11, 17, 19, 21	78–80
		3, 7, 10, 16, 22	82–84
		1, 2, 14, 23	85–86
		20	87–88

CHAPTER 7   THE "SEED" ROOTS

PRETEST
A.

1. accede	4. secede	7. antecede	10. intercede
2. proceed	5. exceed	8. recede	
3. concede	6. succeed	9. supersede	

B.

11. supersede	14. precede	17. exceed	20. recede
12. accede	15. succeed	18. secede	
13. proceed	16. intercede	19. concede	

If you had 18 of 20 correct, you may bypass this chapter. But before you do, find your wrong answers (if any) below, and read the corresponding frames in the chapter so that you will not misspell any words in this test.

Answer numbers	Frames	Answer numbers	Frames
9, 11	2–4	1, 3, 4, 7, 8, 10, 12,	10–33
2, 5, 6, 13, 15, 17	5–7	14, 16, 18, 19, 20	

POSTTEST
A.

1. recede	4. concede	7. supersede	10. antecede
2. exceed	5. accede	8. secede	
3. precede	6. proceed	9. succeed	

B.

11. proceed	13. accede	15. supersede	17. intercede
12. recede	14. precedes	16. exceed	18. concede

For any wrong answer(s) check the frame references below and reread that part of the program. You do not want to leave this chapter without spelling every word in the test correctly.

Answer numbers	Frames	Answer numbers	Frames
7, 15	2–4	4, 5, 13, 18	18–20
2, 6, 9, 11, 16	5–7	17	23–28
3, 14	12–14	10	29
1, 12	15–17	8	33

CHAPTER 8 HOMONYMS

PRETEST

1. compliment		5. coarse		9. stationery		13. too	
2. there		6. principal		10. capitol		14. their	
3. already		7. council		11. cite		15. site	
4. its		8. altogether		12. passed		16. capital	

If you had 14 of 16 correct, you may bypass this chapter. But before you do, find your wrong answers (if any) below, and read the corresponding frames in the chapter so that you will not misspell any words in this test.

Answer numbers	Frames	Answer numbers	Frames
3	1–5	11, 15	34–36
8	6–8	2, 4, 14	38–41
10, 16	13–19	13	42–44
6	20–23	12	48–50
9	24–29	1	51–52
5	30–33	7	53–55

POSTTEST

1. complement		5. all together		9. Capitol		13. consul	
2. its		6. counsel		10. to		14. They're	
3. past		7. sight		11. already		15. Who's	
4. course		8. stationary		12. its		16. principle	

For any wrong answer(s) check the frame references below and reread that part of the program. You do not want to leave this chapter without spelling every word in the test correctly.

Answer numbers	Frames	Answer numbers	Frames
11	1–5	7	34–36
5	6–8	2, 12, 14, 15	38–41
9	13–19	10	42–44
16	20–23	3	48–50
8	24–29	1	51–52
4	30–33	6, 13	53–55

CHAPTER 9 SIMILAR WORDS

PRETEST

1. quite		5. prophesy		9. thorough		13. loose	
2. access		6. accept		10. weather			
3. lose		7. than		11. personnel			
4. casual		8. effects		12. advise			

If you had 11 of 13 correct, you may bypass this chapter. But before you do, find your wrong answers (if any) below, and read the corresponding frames in the chapter so that you will not misspell any words in this test.

Answer numbers	Frames	Answer numbers	Frames
2	1–4	3, 13	25–27
4	5–8	1	28–32
8	9–12	7	34–37
5	13–17	9	38–41
6	18–19	11	42–45
12	21–24	10	46–49

POSTTEST

1. quiet	5. excess	9. prophecy	13. advice
2. whether	6. causal	10. effect	
3. personal	7. accepts	11. then	
4. loose	8. effects	12. whether	

For any wrong answer(s) check the frame references below and reread that part of the program. You do not want to leave this chapter without spelling every word in the test correctly.

Answer numbers	Frames	Answer numbers	Frames
5	1–4	4	25–27
6	5–8	1	28–32
8, 10	9–12	11	34–37
9	13–17	3	42–45
7	18–19	2, 12	46–49

CHAPTER 10   DOUBLING THE FINAL CONSONANT

PRETEST

1. planner	8. beginning	15. instilling	22. chagrined
2. witty	9. occurrence	16. equipped	23. vexing
3. streaked	10. dimly	17. omitted	24. delightful
4. plugger	11. repealed	18. dimmer	25. trafficker
5. taxing	12. transferring	19. excellent	
6. exploiter	13. propellant	20. conference	
7. dropped	14. gossipy	21. benefited	

If you had 22 of 25 correct you may bypass this chapter. But before you do, find your wrong answers (if any) below, and read the corresponding frames in the chapter so that you will not misspell any words in this test.

Answer numbers	Frames	Answer numbers	Frames
1, 2, 3, 4, 5, 7, 10, 18, 23	1–4	12	14
		22	18–20
6, 8, 9, 11, 13, 14, 15, 17, 21, 24	10–11	19, 20	21–27
		25	28–29
16	12		

POSTTEST

1. reference	5. preferring	9. conference	13. chagrining
2. allotter	6. excellence	10. mimicking	14. panicky
3. controlling	7. frolicsome	11. referred	15. visitor
4. galloped	8. beginning	12. rebellion	16. occurrence

17. skimming	20. equipped	23. transferring
18. mimicry	21. relaxed	24. deference
19. difference	22. existence	25. concealed

For any wrong answer(s) check the frame references below and reread that part of the program. You do not want to leave this chapter without spelling every word in the test correctly.

Answer numbers	Frames	Answer numbers	Frames
17	1–4	13	18–20
2, 3, 4, 5, 8, 11, 12,	10–11	1, 6, 9, 24	21–27
15, 16, 19, 21, 22, 25		7, 10, 14, 18	28–29
20	12		
23	14		

CHAPTER 11 THE FINAL *E*

PRETEST

1. desiring	9. argument	17. singeing	25. indispensable
2. useless	10. writing	18. manageable	26. ninth
3. serviceable	11. truly	19. arguing	27. writing
4. duly	12. changeable	20. adventuresome	28. management
5. density	13. wholesome	21. diner	29. accurately
6. advantageous	14. advertisement	22. canoeist	30. dyeing
7. coming	15. losing	23. enforceable	
8. receivable	16. simply	24. wholly	

If you had 27 of 30 correct, you may bypass this chapter. But before you do, find your wrong answer numbers (if any) below, and read the corresponding frames in the chapter so that you will not misspell any words in this test.

Answer numbers	Frames	Answer numbers	Frames
1, 5, 7, 10, 15, 21	1–6	26	15–17
25, 27		9, 19	18–20
3, 6, 8, 12, 18, 23,	7–11	22	22–25
28		17, 30	26–27
2, 13, 14, 20, 29	12–14	4, 11, 16, 24	28–30

POSTTEST

1. achievement	9. judging	17. receiving	25. rarity
2. advisable	10. remoteness	18. density	26. achieving
3. canoeing	11. truly	19. pursuer	27. imaginable
4. pleasurable	12. trueness	20. wholly	28. hoeing
5. manageable	13. singeing	21. changeable	29. argument
6. ageless	14. disadvantaged	22. aching	30. pronounceable
7. canoeist	15. arguing	23. desirous	
8. noticeable	16. simply	24. advantageous	

For any wrong answer(s) check the frame references below and reread that part of the program. You do not want to leave this chapter without spelling every word in the test correctly.

Answer numbers	Frames	Answer numbers	Frames
2, 4, 9, 14, 17, 18,	1–6	15, 29	18–20
19, 22, 23, 25, 26,		3, 7, 28	22–25
27		13	26–27
5, 8, 21, 24, 30	7–11	11, 16, 20	28–30
1, 6, 10, 12	12–14		

CHAPTER 12 THE FINAL Y

PRETEST

1. accompaniment
2. conveys
3. occupying
4. copyist
5. stories
6. burial
7. beauties
8. employer
9. tries
10. tragedies
11. applying
12. happily
13. carrying
14. hungrily
15. beautiful
16. dormitories
17. happiness
18. daily
19. studying
20. pitiful
21. displaying
22. companies
23. pitying
24. cozily
25. chimneys
26. societies
27. trial
28. theories
29. accompanied
30. industries

If you had 27 of 30 correct, you may bypass this chapter. But before you do, find your wrong answer numbers (if any) below, and read the corresponding frames in the chapter so that you will not misspell any words in this test.

Answer numbers	Frames	Answer number	Frames
2, 8, 21, 25	1–4	18	8–13
1, 3, 4, 5, 6, 7, 9,	5–7		
10, 11, 12, 13, 14,			
15, 16, 17, 19, 20,			
22, 23, 24, 26, 27,			
28, 29, 30			

POSTTEST

1. summaries
2. annoyance
3. copier
4. relies
5. portrays
6. defying
7. burial
8. daily
9. paid
10. monkeys
11. societies
12. employed
13. lobbying
14. medleys
15. cemeteries
16. tendencies
17. accompaniment
18. keyed
19. trying
20. laid
21. copyist
22. universities
23. controversies
24. pitiless
25. readying
26. denial
27. luxuries
28. employment
29. said
30. academies

For any wrong answer(s) check the frame references below and reread that part of the program. You do not want to leave this chapter without spelling every word in the test correctly.

Answer numbers	Frames	Answer numbers	Frames
2, 5, 10, 12, 14,	1–4	8, 9, 20, 29	8–13
18, 28			
1, 3, 4, 6, 7, 11,	5–7		
13, 15, 16, 17, 19,			
21, 22, 23, 24, 25,			
26, 27, 30			

CHAPTER 13 *IE OR EI*

PRETEST

1. relieve
2. conceit
3. receive
4. seizure
5. deficient
6. weighed
7. chief
8. piece
9. weird
10. counterfeit
11. height weight
12. achieve
13. foreign
14. neighborhood
15. leisure

If you had 13 of 15 correct, you may bypass this chapter. But before you do, find your wrong answer numbers (if any) below, and read the corresponding frames in the chapter so that you will not misspell any words in this test.

Answer numbers	Frames	Answer numbers	Frames
1, 2, 3, 7, 8, 12	1–7	11	22–25
4, 9, 15	8–11	10, 13	27–35
6, 11, 14	14–21	5	39–47

POSTTEST

1.	believe	5.	receive	9.	yield	13.	thief
2.	siege	6.	forfeit	10.	seize	14.	leisure
3.	sovereign	7.	reindeer	11.	weigh	15.	weird
4.	freight	8.	efficient	12.	deficient		

For any wrong answer(s) check the frame references below and reread that part of the program. You do not want to leave this chapter without spelling every word in the test correctly.

Answer numbers	Frames	Answer numbers	Frames
1, 2, 5, 9, 13	1–7	3, 6	27–35
10, 14, 15	8–11	8, 12	39–47
4, 7, 11	14–21		

CHAPTER 14   PLURALS

PRETEST

1.	displays	9.	Negroes	17.	universities	25.	data
2.	penalties	10.	melodies	18.	Tories	26.	heroes
3.	gases	11.	perches	19.	discrepancies	27.	wives
4.	vetoes	12.	thieves	20.	griefs	28.	studies
5.	zoos	13.	potatoes	21.	halves	29.	decoys
6.	monarchs	14.	Tommys	22.	societies	30.	taxes
7.	inquiries	15.	wishes	23.	gulfs		
8.	crises	16.	buzzes	24.	elegies		

If you had 27 of 30 correct, you may bypass this chapter. But before you do, find your wrong answer numbers (if any) below, and read the corresponding frames in the chapter so that you will not misspell any words in this test.

Answer numbers	Frames	Answer numbers	Frames
3, 6, 11, 15, 16, 23, 30	1–6	4, 5, 9, 13, 26	19–22
1, 2, 7, 10, 17, 19, 22, 24, 28, 29	7–8	12, 20, 21	24–26
		27	27–28
14, 18	9–10	8, 25	31–32

POSTTEST

1.	lives	9.	shelves	17.	bungalows	25.	Henrys
2.	switches	10.	addenda	18.	compresses	26.	epochs
3.	monarchs	11.	photos	19.	crises	27.	Negroes
4.	echoes	12.	treaties	20.	fashions	28.	hypotheses
5.	analyses	13.	tomatoes	21.	data	29.	lobbies
6.	gulches	14.	media	22.	knives	30.	wolves
7.	stereos	15.	Kennedys	23.	deputies		
8.	countries	16.	companies	24.	families		

For any wrong answer(s) check the frame references below and reread that part of the program. You do not want to leave this chapter without spelling every word in the test correctly.

Answer numbers	Frames	Answer numbers	Frames
2, 3, 6, 17, 18, 20, 26	1–6	9, 30	24–26
8, 12, 16, 23, 24, 29	7–8	1, 22	27–28
15, 25	9–10	5, 10, 14, 19, 21, 28	31–32
4, 7, 11, 13, 27	19–22		

CHAPTER 15 POSSESSIVES

PRETEST
1. king's
2. boys'
3. Brannon and Butterworth's
4. John Donne's
5. secretary's and treasurer's
6. women's
7. each other's
8. Louis the Thirteenth's
9. its
10. nobody's
11. friend's
12. father-in-law's
13. minute's

If you had 11 of 13 correct, you may bypass this chapter. But before you do, find your wrong answer numbers (if any) below, and read the corresponding frames in the chapter so that you will not misspell any words in this test.

Answer numbers	Frames	Answer numbers	Frames
1, 2, 4, 6, 11, 13	1–4	3, 5, 8, 12	8–9
7, 9, 10	5–7		

POSTTEST
1. hers
2. others'
3. niece's
4. anybody's
5. sopranos'
6. Day and May's
7. sisters'
8. theirs
9. its
10. runner-up's
11. actresses'
12. men's
13. Mary's
14. brother-in-law's
15. Jack's and Jim's

For any wrong answer(s) check the frame references below and reread that part of the program. You do not want to leave this chapter without spelling every word in the test correctly.

Answer numbers	Frames	Answer numbers	Frames
3, 5, 7, 11, 12, 13	1–4	6 10, 14, 15	8–9
1, 2, 4, 8, 9	5–7		

CHAPTER 16 LY AND OUS

PRETEST
A. *ly-ally*
1. basically
2. morally
3. truly
4. frequently
5. continuously
6. publicly
7. accidentally
8. angrily
9. chiefly
10. duly
11. finally
12. accurately
13. vaguely
14. wholly
15. easily
16. coyly
17. dryly or drily
18. safely
19. simply
20. slyly

B. ous

21. various	24. mischievous	27. mountainous	30. grievous
22. perilous	25. libelous	28. adventurous	31. victorious
23. advantageous	26. piteous	29. troublous	32. spacious

If you had 18 of 20 in A and 10 of 12 in B correct, you may bypass this chapter. But before you do, find your wrong answer numbers (if any) below, and read the corresponding frames in the chapter so that you will not misspell any words in this test.

Answer numbers	Frames	Answer numbers	Frames
A.		B.	
2, 4, 5, 7, 9, 11	1–3	22, 24, 25, 27, 30	22–23
3, 10, 12, 13, 14,	4–6	23, 28, 29, 32	24–25
18, 19		21, 26, 31	26–29
8, 15, 16, 17, 20	7–10		
1, 6	15		

POSTTEST

A. ly-ally

1. really	6. finally	11. academically	16. perceptibly
2. angrily	7. publicly	12. entirely	17. drastically
3. truly	8. hungrily	13. simply	18. duly
4. shyly or shily	9. apologetically	14. likely	19. trickily
5. certainly	10. wholly	15. tastily	20. slyly

B. ous

21. grievous	24. courageous	27. ridiculous	20. riotous
22. desirous	25. gracious	28. bounteous	31. injurious
23. hazardous	26. plenteous	29. dangerous	32. mischievous

For any wrong answer(s) check the frame references below and reread that part of the program. You do not want to leave this chapter without spelling every word in the test correctly.

Answer numbers	Frames	Answer numbers	Frames
A.		B.	
1, 5, 6	1–3	21, 23, 29, 30, 32	22–23
3, 10, 12, 13, 14	4–6	22, 24, 25, 27	24–25
18		26, 28, 31	26–29
2, 4, 8, 15, 19, 20	7–10		
16	12–14		
7, 9, 11, 17	15–16		

APPENDIX A   GUIDELINES FOR SYLLABICATION

PRETEST

1. nec es sar y	11. ref er ence
2. man u fac ture	12. ac cu mu late
3. vow el	13. de lude
4. ac com mo date	14. pi lot
5. car pen ter	15. soph o more
6. rap id	16. an ti bod y
7. con sid er a tion	17. con so nant
8. an tip a thy	18. ap pear ance
9. ge ol o gy	19. trib u la tion
10. rub ble	20. ri val ry

If you had 18 of 20 correct, you may bypass this section.

POSTTEST

1. con tro ver sy
2. res tau rant
3. re cur rence
4. pre cede
5. dis ap point ment
6. tre men dous
7. un nec es sar y
8. de scrip tion
9. op por tu ni ty
10. ad van tage ous

11. in ci den tal
12. doc u men ta ry
13. knowl edge
14. Wed nes day
15. psy chol o gy
16. ri dic u lous
17. a chieve ment
18. for got ten
19. gov ern ment
20. pro ce dure

If you missed any, reread frames 13–24 and 30–34 so that you will not leave this part of the program without dividing every word in the test correctly.

Index

a:
   long sound cf, 134–135,
      171–172
   plural form of Latin
      nouns, 148–149
   short sound of, 171
   unstressed vowel problem,
      45
able, words ending in,
   53–59
Abundance, 66–67
Accede, 75
Accent in words, 173–175
   (See also Stress)
Accept-except, 94
Acceptance, 63
Access-excess, 92
Accommodate, 177
Accompanies, 126
Accomplishment, 23
Accumulatc, 23
Achieve, 132–133
Acquaintance, 28
Acquire, 28
Admirable, 53–54
Admissible, 53–54
Adolescent, 64–65
Advantageous, 116, 164
Advertise, 61
Advice-advise, 94
Affect-effect, 93
Aggravate, 10
All ready-already, 80–81

All right-alright, 81
All together-altogether, 81
Analyses, 148–149
Analyze, 61–62
ance, words ending in,
   63–69
Antecede, 76
Antecedent, 66–67
Apparent, 24
Appreciate, 23–24
Argument, 118
Arise, 60–61
ary, words ending in, 59–60
Athlete, athletics, 4
Attendance, 66–67

Background, 8–9
Balance, 65–66
Beauteous, 164–165
Beginning, 106–107
Benefit, 45–46
Benefited, 107
Boundary, 59
Brilliant, 67
Bulletin, 45–46

c:
   hard sound of: in words
      ending in able-ible,
      56–57
   in words ending in
      ance-ence, 64–65

c:
  soft sound of: in words
      ending in *able-ible*,
      56–57, 116–117
    in words ending in
      ance-ence, 64–65
    in words ending in *ous*,
      164
Calendar, 43–44
Candidate, 47
Canoeing, 119–120
Capital-capitol-Capitol, 82
Casual-causal, 92–93
Category, 45–46
cede, ceed, sede endings,
      73–78
    cede, 75–77
    ceed, 74
    posttest, 78
    pretest, 73
    sede, 74
    (See *also* specific words
      entries)
Cemetery, 59, 143
Chagrin, 109
Changeable, 56–57, 116
Characterize, 61, 63
Chimney, 5–6
cient, words ending in,
      137–139
Cite-sight-site, 84–85
Coarse-course, 84
Comparative, 45
Competence, 63–64
Complement-compliment, 88
Concede, 75
Condemn, 38
Conference, 109
Confidence, 66–67
Consequent, 67–68
Consistence, 63–64
Consonants:
    difficulty with double,
      22–28
    final, doubling before
      suffix, 103–112
    in syllabication, 174–175

Consonants:
    words ending in, before
      ous, 163–164
Consul-council-counsel,
      88–89
Contemporary, 59
Contractions mistaken for
      possessives, 86, 154
Controversy, 46
Convenience, 31, 67
Council-counsel-consul,
      88–89
Counterfeit, 136–137
Courageous, 164
Course-coarse, 84
Crises, 148–149
Criticism, 48
Criticize, 61–63

Data, 148–149
Debt, 36
Defendant, 66–67
Defensible, 55
Deference, 109
Deficient, 138–139
Definite, 47
Delinquent, 67–68
Dependent, 66–67
Descendant, 66–67
Describe, 14
Desirous, 114
Dipthongs, 171–172
Disappear, 26
Disappoint, 26
Disapprove, 14
Disastrous, 5
Discrimination, 25–26
Dispensable, 55
Dissatisfaction, 25
Dissect, 14
Dissent, 14
Divide, 42
Dominance, 65–66
Dominant, 47
Dormitory, 48
Doubling final consonant
      (see Final consonant)

Doubt, 36
Duly, 121, 160–161
Dyeing, 120

e:
   final, before *ly,* 117–118,
     121, 160–161
   long sound of, 132–134,
     171–172
   before most suffixes,
     113–122
   short sound of, 171
   unstressed vowel problem,
     45–46
Echoes, 146–147
Educable, 56–57
Effect-affect, 93
Efficient, 137–139
ei-ie (see *ie-ei*)
Either, 133–134
Eligible, 56–57
Eliminate, 48
Embarrass, 27
Emergence, 64–65
Eminence, 65–66
Emphasize, 61–62
ence, words ending in,
   63–69
Enforceable, 56–57, 117
Enterprise, 61
Enunciation of words (*see*
   Mispronunciation of
   words)
Environment, 8
Equip, 107–108
Equivalent, 65–66
ery, words ending in, 59–60
Evitable, 54–55
Exceed, 74
Excellence, 65–66
Except-accept, 94
Excess-access, 92
Exercise, 60–61
Exhaust, 37
Existence, 63–64
Experience, 30–31, 67
Explanation, 29–30

Extravagance, 64–65

f, fe, ff, plural of words
   ending in, 147–148
Familiar, 44
Fascinate, 47
February, 59
Federal, 7
Final consonant:
   doubling before suffix,
     103–112
   posttest, 112
   pretest, 103
   words of one syllable,
     104–106
   words of two or more
     syllables, 106–110
   ending in single vowel
     and consonant with
     accented last
     syllable, 106–109
   exceptions, 109, 110
   shift in stress, 109–
     110
Final e, 113–122
   dropping before suffix,
     114–116
   keeping before suffix:
     beginning with a
     consonant, 117–119
     in *dye* and *singe,* 120
     exceptions, 118–119,
     121–122
     in words ending in oe,
     119–120
     in words with soft
     sound of c or g,
     116–117
   posttest, 122
   pretest, 112
Final y, 123–130
   changing to i before
     suffix, 125–128
   keeping before suffix,
     124–125
   posttest, 129–130
   pretest, 123–124

Final *y*:
  (See *also* Plurals)
Finally, 8, 160
Financier, 32
Foreign, 136–137
Forfeit, 136–137
Freight, 134–135

g:
  hard sound of: in words
     ending in *able-ible*,
     56–57
    in words ending in
     ance-ence, 64
  soft sound of: in words
     ending in *able-ible*,
     56–57, 116–117
    in words ending in
     ance-ence, 64
    in words ending in *ous*,
     116–117, 164–165
Government, 8
Gracious, 164
Grammar, 43–44
Gratitude, 9–10
Grievous, 4–5, 163–164
Guard-guardian, 39
Guidance, 66–67, 115
Guidelines for syllabication,
  169–178
  generalizations, 174–176
  one consonant between
    two vowels: with
    long accented first
    vowel, 174
    with short accented
    first vowel, 175
  pronunciation and
    syllabication, 175–
    176
  two consonants be-
    tween two vowels,
    175
    words ending in *le*, 175
  posttest, 178
  pretest, 170

Guidelines for syllabication:
  sounds: letters represent-
    ing, 170
    vowel, 171–172
  stress, major and minor,
    173
  syllable, definition of,
    172–173

h, semivowel, 170–172
Height, 136
Heroes, 146–147
Hindrance, 5
Homonyms, 79–90
  posttest, 90
  pretest, 79
  (See *also* specific word
    entries)
Horrible, 53
Humorous, 46
Hundred, 10

i:
  long sound of, 136, 171
  short sound of, 136–137,
    171
  unstressed vowel problem,
    47–49
ible, words ending in, 53–59
ie-ei, 131–139
  posttest, 139
  pretest, 131
  sound: of long *a*, 134–
    135
    of long *e*, 132–134
    of long *i*, 136
    of *sh* (*cie*), 137–139
    of short *i*, 136–137
Immediately, 26
Imminence, 65–66
Independence, 66–67
Inevitable, 54–55
Influence, 67–68
Ingredient, 67–68
Insistence, 63–64
Intelligence, 48–49, 64–65

Intercede, 76
Interest, 31
Interrupt, 29
Irrelevant, 28
ise-ize-yze, words ending in, 60–63
It's-its, 86

Knives, 148
Know-no, 87
Knowledge, 37

Laboratory, 46
Laid, 127
Legible, 56–57
Legitimate, 48
Leisure, 133–134
Liable, 6–7
Library, 59
Lightening, 6
Lightning, 5–6
Loneliness, 29
Loose-lose, 95
ly, 159–163
   with most words, 160
   posttest, 166
   pretest, 159
   with words ending in *ble*, 162
   with words ending in final e, 160–161
   with words ending in final y, 161–162
   with words ending in *ic*, 162–163

Magnificence, 64–65
Maintenance, 65–66
Mandatory, 45
Mathematics, 45–46
Media, 148–149
Merchandise, 61
Mimic, 110
Mischievous, 4–5, 163–164

Mispronunciation of words, results of, 3–12
   addition of syllable, 4–6
   omission of syllable or letter, 6–9
   posttest, 11
   pretest, 3
   substitution of wrong letters, 9–11

Negroes, 146–147
Neither, 133–134
Ninety, 118
Ninth, 118
No-know, 87
Noticeable, 56–57, 116–117

o:
   long sound of, 171
   plural of nouns ending in, 146–147
   short sound of, 171
   unstressed vowel problem, 46–47
Occasionally, 24
Occurrence, 106–107
Opinion, 42–43
Opportunity, 24
Optimism, 48
ous, 163–166
   posttest, 166
   pretest, 160
   with words ending in a consonant, 163–164
   with words ending in *f*, 163–164
   with words ending in *ge* and *ce*, 164–165
   with words ending in *y*, 164–165

Paid-payed, 127–128
Panic, 110
Parallel, 27

Paralyze, 61–62
Particular, 43
Passed-past, 87–88
Peculiar, 44
Perfectible, 53–54
Perform, 15
Permanent, 65–66
Permissible, 53–54
Persistence, 63–64
Personal-personnel, 97–98
Picnic, 110
Piteous, 164–165
Pitiable, 53
Plurals, 141–150
  general formation of, 142
  of Latin nouns, 148–149
  of nouns ending in *ch, s,*
    sh, tch, x, z, 142–143
  of nouns ending in *f, fe,*
    ff, 147–148
  of nouns ending in *o,*
    146–147
  of nouns ending in *y,*
    143–145
  posttest, 150
  pretest, 141
Possession, 26
Possessive form, 151–158
  of compound nouns, 154–
    155
  of indefinite pronouns,
    153–154
  of nouns not ending in *s,*
    152–153
  the "of phrase," 155–156
  of personal pronouns,
    153–154
  of plural nouns ending in
    s, 152–153
  posttest, 157–158
  pretest, 151–152
Possible, 53
Potatoes, 146–147
Precede, 15, 75
Prefixes, 13–19
  de-dis, 14–15
  mis-dis-un, 17–18
  posttest, 19

Prefixes:
  pre-per-pro, 15–16
  pretest, 13–14
  re, 17
  (See *also* specific word
    entries)
Prejudice, 10–11
Prevalent, 65–66
Principal-principle, 82–83
Privilege, 49
Probably, 45
Procedure, 29–30
Proceed, 74
Proficient, 137–138
Prominence, 65–66
Pronunciation of words (see
  Mispronunciation of
  words)
Prophecy-prophesy, 93–94
Propose, 15
Psychiatry, 38–39
Psychology, 38–39
Publicly, 162–163

Quantity, 7
Quiet-quite, 95

Realize, 61–62
Recede, 75
Receive, 132–133
Recognize, 10, 61–63
Recollect, 17
Recommend, 17
Reference, 109
Referred, 107
Reign, 135
Relevance, 63
Reliable, 53
Remembrance, 5
Repressible, 53–55
Responsible, 55
Restaurant, 32
Revocable, 56–57
Rhythm, 37
Ridiculous, 42

Sacrifice, 49
Science, 67–68
Secede, 77
Secretary, 59
sede ending (see *cede, ceed, sede* endings)
Seize-seizure, 133–134
Semivowels, 170–172
Sentence, 44
Separate, 45
Sergeant, 32
Serviceable, 56–57, 116
sh sound written as *cie,* 137–139
Sight-site-cite, 84–85
Significance, 64–65
Silent letters in words, 35–40
    posttest, 35
    pretest, 40
Similar, 43–44
Similar words, 91–99
    posttest, 99
    pretest, 91
Simply, 121, 160–161
Singeing, 120
Sovereign, 136–137
Spacious, 164
Stationary-stationery, 59, 83
Stress:
    of vowels (see Vowel stress in words)
    in words: definition of, 173
        kinds of, 173
        shift in, 109–110
Studying, 126–127
Subtle, 36
Succeed, 74
Sufficient, 137–138
Suffixes, 51–70
    able-ible, 53–59
    ance-ence, 63–69
    ary-ery, 59–60
    ise-ize-yze, 60–63
    posttest, 69–70
    pretest, 51–52

Suffixes:
    (See *also* specific word entries)
Summarize, 61, 63
Superintendent, 66–67
Supersede, 74
Supervise, 61
Surfeit, 136–137
Surprise, 60–61
Syllabication:
    five-step method, 22–23
    graphic presentation of (see Guidelines for syllabication)
    posttest, 33–34
    prefixes in, 28–29
    pretest, 21–22
    pronunciation, analysis, and, 21, 28–32
    suffixes in, 29–31
    of words of French derivation, 32–33

Temperament, 7
Temperature, 7
Than-then, 96
Their-there-they're, 86
Thorough-through, 97
To-too-two, 86–87
Traffic, 110
Tragedy, 10–11
Transfer, 108
Truly, 121, 160–161

u:
    long sound of, 171
    short sound of, 171
Undoubtedly, 36
Usage, 117

Vacuum, 31–32
Variable, 53
Various, 164–165
Vegetable, 7
Vetoes, 146–147

Villain, 31
Vowel sounds, 171–172
Vowel stress in words,
    41–50
  posttest, 50
  pretest, 41–42
  slight, 42
  unstressed: in first
      syllable, 42–43
    in last syllable, 43–44
    in middle of word,
      45–49
      a problem, 45
      e problem, 45–46
      i problem, 47–49
      o problem, 46–47

w, semivowel, 170–172
Warrant, 43
Weather-whether, 98
Wednesday, 36–37

Weigh, 134–135
Weird, 133–134
Who's-whose, 86
Wholly, 121, 160–161
Wives, 148
Words, similar in appear-
    ance or sound (*see*
    Similar words)
Writing, 39, 114

y, final: before *able*, 53
    before *ly*, 125–127,
      161–162
    before most suffixes,
      124–128
    before *ous*, 164–165
    plural of nouns ending
      in, 143–145
    semivowel, 170–172
You're-your, 86
yze, words ending in, 60–63